ESSAYS ON OPERA

EGON WELLESZ

ESSAYS ON OPERA

Translated from the German by
PATRICIA KEAN

London
DENNIS DOBSON LTD

First published in Great Britain in MCML by
DENNIS DOBSON LTD, 12 Park Place, St
James's, London SW1. Translated from the German
by *Patricia Kean*. All rights reserved. Printed in
Great Britain by the BRISTOL TYPESETTING
CO, Stokes Croft, Bristol.
132/R

CONTENTS

Preface 7

I The Beginning of Baroque in Music . . . 13

II The Beginnings of Opera in Vienna . . . 33

III Italian Musicians at the Austrian Court . . 46

IV A Festival Opera of the Seventeenth Century . 54

V The *Balletto a Cavallo* 82

VI Three Lectures on Opera 90

    (a) The Problem of Form 90

    (b) Music Drama 106

    (c) The Latest Development of Opera . . 123

VII The Idea of the Heroic and Opera . . . 140

VIII *Alkestis* 145

IX *Opferung des Gefangenen* 153

PREFACE

THIS VOLUME CONSISTS of a selection of articles, lectures and addresses, all of which are concerned with opera. They all date from the time when I was living in Vienna. They all give expression to my lifelong interest in the problem of Opera, to begin with as a historian of music, later as a composer.

For a musician who comes from Vienna where the tradition of opera goes back for four hundred years, opera as a form of art has a special meaning. For him it is not a hybrid genre inferior to spoken drama, as it seems to so many musicians of other countries who only occasionally hear an opera and who are so disturbed by the complexity of the experience that they cannot comprehend what they see and hear as a self-contained unity. Opera is for the composer a world within the world in which everything takes place in accordance with the laws proper to this form of art. Through the music the action is raised into a sphere in which the composer gives finality to the words.

The characters of the actors in the drama are developed through the line of the melody and through the orchestration of the music which accompanies the singing. When the words end the music forms a bridge. From the earliest operas of Monteverdi onwards we see the composer trying to create something raised above the level of everyday life, and every reform of opera aims at a perfect equilibrium of words and music, and a treatment of the stage that will leave the hearer free to concentrate on the essentials of the action.

In my youth in Vienna I saw performances of the highest

perfection, as far as production, music and décor were concerned, at the Vienna Court Opera under Gustav Mahler. One of my strongest impressions was the performance of Gluck's *Iphigenia in Aulis*. I began to concern myself with Gluck's reform of opera and as subject for a thesis I chose the operas and oratorios of Giuseppe Bonno, one of Gluck's contemporaries. From him my studies led me to the beginnings of opera, to Monteverdi and Cavalli, and to the great change in music which was brought about by the development of a new style in Italy and in those countries which were under Italian influence.

The first essay in the present volume, 'The Beginning of Baroque in Music,' deals with the characteristics of the new style. It appeared in a first draft forty years ago, in 1909, in the *Zeitschrift der Internationalen Musikgesellschaft*, vol. xi. An enlarged version appeared in 1922 as the first part of a booklet in the series *Theater und Kultur* (Vienna). Though much has been written lately on the subject,[1] I felt it desirable to make few changes and to leave the essay as an expression of my point of view at the time when it was written. The term 'Baroque' has been used in recent books on the history of music for a whole period of European art and in this sense it has seemed to many historians of music in this country too general to be of use. I have limited myself to defining the two terms 'Baroque' and 'Renaissance,' and restricted my inquiry to Italian music in which the same signs of a new way of expression are to be found as in Italian architecture and sculpture.

The next essay, 'The Beginnings of Opera in Vienna,' was first printed as the second part of the same booklet in 1922. Working in the music department of the National Library in Vienna I went through the scores and libretti of all the cantatas, operas and oratorios which were performed between 1691 and 1770. This essay gives a brief survey of this period. The study 'Italian Musicians at the Austrian

---

[1] Notably P. H. Lang, *Music in Western Civilization*; M. Bukofzer, *Music in the Baroque Era*; A. Einstein, *The Italian Madrigal*.

Court' first appeared in 1940 in the *Monthly Musical
Record*, though it was written earlier in Vienna and the translation has been revised for the present book. It adds some
details confirming the dominating rôle played by Italian musicians in Austria in the seventeenth century. This predominance
is further illustrated by an essay, ' A Festival Opera of the
Seventeenth Century ' first published in 1914 in *Die Musik*,
which gives a detailed description of Marc' Antonio Cesti's *Il
pomo d'oro*, composed for the wedding celebrations of the
Emperor Leopold I and Margareta Theresia of Spain in 1666.
The performance of *Il pomo d'oro* is a landmark in the history
of Italian opera; it is as a matter of fact one of the first grand
operas of the Venetian school and its performance was a
perfect blending of words, music and production. The opera
was preceded some days before by a *Balletto a Cavallo* of
which we possess the libretto, the full score, and a description
of the performance in the *Diarium Europaeum*. The essay in
this book is based on a study ' Die Ballett-Suiten von J. H.
und A. A. Schmelzer,' which I published in the *Sitzungs-
berichte der Akademie der Wissenschaften in Wien* in 1914.
It is the translation of an article, ' Das Balletto a Cavallo '
written for *Der Anbruch* in 1928.

This group of essays makes up the first part of the book. I
included only studies on operas on which I have done some
original research and I did not include any of my studies on
eighteenth-century opera since they are of merely musico-
logical interest. The last of these, ' Die Opern und Oratorien
in Wien von 1660-1708,' was published in the sixth volume
of the *Studien zur Musikwissenschaft* (Vienna) in 1919. This
date coincides with the composition of my first opera, *Die
Prinzessin Girnara*, and the beginnings of my studies in
Byzantine music.

The omission of any essay on Gluck among the studies on
Baroque opera perhaps needs a word of explanation. What I
have to say about him is beyond the scope of a short essay
of the type which makes up this book, and this will be clear
if my own development as scholar and composer is taken

into account; my researches on opera before Gluck were immediately followed by the composition of my own operas: the importance of Gluck to these will be apparent from the concluding essays. I consider Gluck as the last composer to follow the Austrian Baroque tradition, and at the same time an innovator whose particular line was not taken up in Vienna. I felt that to renew the Austrian operatic tradition I had to go back to this new line of Gluck's. But here I must leave the reader to turn to the essays on my own operas.

The second part of the book contains the three lectures on opera which I delivered at the Royal College of Music, the Royal Academy of Music and Trinity College of Music for the University of London in October and November, 1933. The years between 1918 and 1931 were those of my own activities as a dramatic composer; activities which were favoured by the great interest in contemporary operatic pro- ductions all over the Continent, but particularly in Germany. In England, I felt at the time, interest in opera was growing among musicians and music lovers, but composers were not given the chance of a good training in dramatic composi- tion, as they were on the Continent. These three lectures, therefore, were intended to make the music students of the three colleges acquainted with the various tendencies in opera and to throw some light upon the social conditions which favoured the growth of opera on the Continent.

The last three essays are concerned with my own operatic works. 'The Idea of the Heroic and Opera' is based on a paper which I read in 1928 to an audience in the Theatre of Gera on the day before the first performance of my own opera *Alkestis*. It was published in the *Jahrbuch der Reus- sischen Theaters*. *Alkestis* is based on a talk given in Cologne in 1926, again before the performance of the opera; the last one, an introductory note to the 'Sacrifice of the Prisoner,' first appeared in 1926 in 'Die Musikblätter des Anbruch.' I included these essays because they contain the essence of my own views on opera. I hope they are not merely of historical value since two of my operas seem to have survived the catastrophe through which so many works have disappeared from the repertory.

When it was decided to publish the *Essays on Opera,* I went carefully through all of them, eliminating passages and sections which were written only with reference to a particular occasion, or which overlapped with other parts of the book. The last three essays on my own works have been completely reshaped. Miss Patricia Kean translated those essays which were originally written in German. I wish to express my gratitude for the help she gave me in the task of revising the text of the essays and in suggesting to me an adequate rendering of German technical terms which have no equivalent in English. Both author and translator have co-operated in an effort to make this collection of essays a readable book for the wide public interested in opera in this country.

It is, indeed, encouraging to see how much things have changed in this country during the last years. The confidence in the growth of operatic life in England which I expressed in the last of my London lectures in 1933 was justified and we can now hope that opera will soon flourish in this country.

I

The Beginning of Baroque in Music

i

To DIVIDE UP a period of artistic development by means of dates is always an arbitrary proceeding. It is to assume a final point, a place of rest, where everything is in a constant state of flux and motion. And yet limitation is necessary if we are to orientate ourselves in the immense variety of the phenomena which make up the history of art, and for this reason sections must be marked off in time, the periods of art history.

In order to obtain more easily a general view of the separate periods, we are accustomed to refer to them by names which are intended to sum them up and to distinguish them accurately from each other. These names have been handed down and accepted without criticism for a long time now, though they are by no means fitted for the use to which they are put. They are not the result of critical reflection, but have been thrown up by chance and crystallized into formulæ. They are either entirely misapplied, like 'Gothic' in the derogatory sense of 'barbaric art' in which it was used by Vasari, or they only fit a single one among a variety of movements to which they are applied, like 'Renaissance' which applies to the rebirth of Classicism. Or else they express an adverse judgement like 'Baroque' which, though its etymology is still uncertain, was very early connected with *barocco,* a term applied to painting meaning an excessive emotionalism, as in the case of some of the followers of Michelangelo.

These terms were first employed for systematic classification in the Romantic period. If we wish to use them nowadays as aids to the study of the history of art we must not expect them to provide an explanation of the phenomena but must consider them only as conventional fictions, coined to aid our understanding.

Since they belonged to a period in which the study of history was still essentially concerned with the description of facts, these terms could hardly be adequate to a period in which it had advanced to the idea of a continuous development in the realm of cultural activity.

But it was only when the individual work of art was no longer considered in isolation, when its relationship to the other works of its time was investigated, its antecedents explored, and all the tangled threads followed out until every connection was laid bare, that it was possible to form a fair judgement of the works of the past. It then became necessary to subject the ideas which were associated with the terms Gothic, Renaissance, Baroque, and Rococo to a revision, because the limits of the periods designated by them had shifted.

This modification is particularly striking in the case of the terms Baroque and Renaissance. Before Jacob Burckhardt wrote, Gothic had to lend its name to part of what we now call the art of the Renaissance, and it is to a great extent his achievement to have set the beginning of the Renaissance further back. But Burckhardt went too far in his conclusions, with the result that he valued this period too highly and too one-sidedly, while his judgement of the preceding Gothic and the following Baroque period suffered.

Once the prevailing idea of a period of outstanding achievement, complete and isolated, had been overcome it was possible to rediscover the Renaissance. It is an outstanding period, in so far as it solves all the problems of an earlier age and gives them a new impulse through its re-orientation to the ancient world. But from the point of view of the hidden forces which determined the development, the Renaissance is a period of transition, standing between Gothic, which still belongs to the Middle Ages, and Baroque which already belongs to the modern period. The germ of a new art had already begun to stir in it, and it was to lead to entirely new artistic problems. In painting, for example, to the problem of the treatment of light and space; in architecture to the problem of the unification of space in a design, to the use of light and shade to produce illusion, to the invasion of plastic art by painting. In music it is the final overthrow of the *cantus firmus* and, connected with this, the emergence of the highest part to bear the melody; the organized use of successions of chords, which are subjected to the laws of tension and relaxation, through which the evolution of new forms was first made possible; the penetration of the melodic line by *fiorituri*; the emergence of a characteristic way of writing for the instruments, and with it the beginnings of the use of orchestral colour. If we take all these phenomena together, they mean nothing else but the beginning of the subjective in music.

Events of far-reaching importance in the political, religious, and economic spheres mark the beginning of the new period which we call Baroque, and which has been an active influence, creative in the highest degree up to the present day. We may place the beginning of the new Baroque feeling in art in the fifteen-twenties. As the result of the discoveries and experiences of the preceding period, and of the economic developments which were bound up with them, many new values had arisen in the world of ideas, which, in art, led to new forms and new problems.

The home of the new movement was the centre of what was then the cultivated world, Rome, and the towns of central Italy.

Born in a violent and eventful age, the new art took as its subject the titanic—the Italians speak of ' *il stile colossale* '— the eternally moved which presses outward beyond its own boundaries, and it held to this principle throughout the greater part of two centuries. It was only gradually, as the aspirations of the cultured world changed, and turned to the ideal of the return to nature, that the external form of this style altered, and that, in place of the heroic and the dynamic of Baroque emerged the grace and delicacy of Rococo. This did not mean a break with the essential ideas of the preceding period, only an emotional change.

Recently it has become the custom to apply the terms Gothic, Renaissance, Baroque, Rococo and Classical not only to the periods with which they were originally associated but wherever similar phenomena are to be found. Thus we speak of a 'classical Rococo,' a 'classical Baroque' and a 'Carolingian Renaissance.' It seems to me that there is a certain danger in this; that terms like these which, as we have seen, are only to be used by necessity and in full recognition of their inadequacy, should now become part of the general terminology of the history of art.

But perhaps the following remarks may be of use to point the antithesis between Renaissance and Baroque.

From the Ancient World onwards two streams can be traced which have persisted without intermission; an individualizing and a generalizing tendency. The individualizing tendency, in which the individual will is predominant, is subjective. The generalizing, in which the collective experience comes into play, is objective. For the individualizing tendency content is more important than form. For the generalizing, form is more important than content. In the former all is in a state of evolution and movement; in the latter all is fixed and at rest. In the individualizing tendency content shatters old forms and creates new; in the generalizing, forms harden and compel the content to adapt itself to them. The individualizing tendency confuses the means proper to the separate arts. The generalizing stands for clarity and unity.

The continued co-existence of these two which only seem to follow each other in time, can easily be overlooked if the attention is only directed to the masterpieces of the art of any period. But from an adequate investigation of the whole artistic activity it will always be found that where one tendency emerges as the main stream of the period the other will always be there as the secondary stream. In transitional periods both flow, either equally strong, side by side, or, coming to the surface in rapid succession, they imitate in miniature the successions which constitute the longer periods. Whichever tendency was the ruling one in a given period will in the next be carried on eclectically, as the secondary stream until, in a new altered form, it again takes the lead.

ii

The creation of larger forms in music, up to the Baroque period, was bound up with the existence of constructive means. But from the moment when the leading part became also the upper part—melody in our sense—the great revolution in music began. The melody came to express emotion with embellishments and coloratura, and therefore gained such importance that all other parts had to subordinate themselves to it. From this it follows that it was still necessary to compose these subordinate parts with as much care as before, but it is no longer the progression of parts which is important, but the accord of the accompanying parts with the melody. The harmonic element which had arisen from the variety of the ecclesiastical modes through the introduction of accidentals comes into the foreground, and it tended more and more towards the clear contrasts of major and minor. The chords are carefully chosen and linked together. Dissonance becomes a means of heightening the harmonic effect. Now for the first time music is freed from the restriction of a form imposed from outside. The first stage was passed in the development of polyphony, and now it was equally necessary to begin again from the beginning. In its turn the instrumental music written at the beginning of the sixteenth century appeared primitive and crude in comparison with works in the old style. But it is the beginning of a new way of writing based on the qualities of the instruments, the beginning of an instrumental structure and a thematic treatment distinct from that of vocal music. If for example we glance at the music of the lutenists we will be

B

struck by the incoherence of the progression of parts, but if we hear it we will realize that the method of composition is conditioned by the technical and sonorous possibilities of the instrument.

The advance, or rather the development of music is dearly bought, for under the influence of this new development in style, the splendid achievement of the *a capella* singing lost ground during the sixteenth century and in the course of the seventeenth gradually vanished. A similar process is to be observed in the eighteenth century: here it is the highly developed contrapuntal style which is sacrificed to the growing power of symphonic writing. And at the present day we ourselves can see how, in its turn, this style, which was brought to such perfection by the orchestral composers of the nineteenth century, is in process of being displaced by a new tendency which renounces the high achievement of the orchestral style for a new primitive mode of expression, just as monody renounced the riches of the *a capella* style.

In histories of music the revolutionary change which was brought about by the replacement of polyphonic choral singing by one-part, monodic singing was not until recently given due weight. To an understanding of art which was biased by the so-called 'classical' idea of beauty this movement was entirely foreign. The real beginning of Baroque in music was, therefore, overlooked, and the appearance of music-drama was considered to be the decisive point of the development. Goldschmidt in the *Lehre von der vokalen Ornamentik*, Leichtentritt in the revised edition of the fourth volume of Ambros's *Geschichte der Musik*, Riemann in the *Handbuch der Musikgeschichte* II, 2, and Adler in the *Stil der Musik*, were the first to form an historically objective judgement of the monodic style. But a comprehensive account of the period is still lacking. It ought not to restrict itself to the music alone, but to take into account all the factors which brought about this radical change in the sphere of aesthetics. It must in fact be put upon the broad basis of the history of civilization.

The history of music itself has not fully utilized the primary

sources at its disposal. For, besides the actual musical works
which have been preserved either in manuscript or in print,
the prefaces of composers to their works, and the treatises of
the theorists must be taken into consideration, for they have
for the most part in this period lost their earlier more theor-
etical character and are concerned with the philosophy of art.
The time has come for a systematic examination of these
sources, so that a complete picture may be obtained of this
exceptionally important period.

iii

The struggle for the supremacy of the new tendency lasted
throughout almost the whole of the sixteenth century. It is
not only the new forms which are filled with its spirit; the old
ones, too, were affected by the impulse towards greater expressiveness. In polyphony also, the free ornamentation of the
separate parts was usual, with the result that each singer tried
to outdo the rest and orderly singing degenerated into a wild
confusion of parts. This destruction of choral singing by the
use of the new methods did not, however, discredit the new
movement, but was used as proof of the imperfection of
singing in the old contrapuntal style.

The development of monodic singing was carried through
in a systematic and interesting way. Monody begins when, in
a polyphonic work, the highest part, and the highest part only,
is ornamented. It is thus distinguished technically and
aesthetically from the other parts, which become less important
and are no longer performed by singers but by instruments.
Here two courses are open. Each part may be taken by
separate instruments or they may all be rendered together in
the manner of a piano arrangement, by organ, clavichord, or
lute. The arrangement was particularly popular at this period.
It made it possible for an amateur, alone and unrestricted,
to perform works which, up to now, had needed four or five
musicians. When this method of adaptation had been in use
for a time works began to be written for such settings without

recourse to the intermediate stage of the arrangement. In these compositions the independence of the accompanying parts became more and more reduced. The whole attention was now concentrated on the development of the solo-voice part. The emergence of the *basso generale* or *basso continuo,* provided the most important technical means to the construction of monody. It used to be thought that it was discovered by Lodovico Grossi da Viadana after 1600, but this view has been long ago abandoned since a number of works with *basso continuo* existed as early as the end of the sixteenth century.

Here, an innovation in notation must be mentioned, which later had a great influence on the essential structure of the work. When the parts which accompanied the leading vocal part had lost their independent life to such an extent that we can no longer speak of parts, but only of accompanying chords, the composer simplified the writing out of his score by only putting down the vocal part and the instrumental bass, leaving it to the instrumentalist to fill in the harmonies of the middle parts. In this, however, he was guided as to the intentions of the composer by figures set under the bass part.

The monodic style was, then, towards the end of the seventeenth century capable, with its expressive melodic technique, of embodying passionate feeling and was ready to join itself to a new kind of lyric as it later actually did in the cantata when the appearance of the music drama gave it another direction.

The drama had been prepared for music by the *intermedii* and by the religious drama. It was given the final impulses through the endeavour of a circle of learned men to revive Greek tragedy with singing and acting.

The oldest example of music inserted in a spoken drama is the pieces of music in Poliziano's *Orfeo* of 1471, and it is noteworthy that they were placed where the dramatic tension was highest. It is not without interest to recall that even when the *dramma per musica* with its complete musical setting had evolved, theorists like Doni held that it was better only to set the crises of the action to music, not the whole drama.

From 1480, when a *Conversione di S. Paolo* was performed, it became the established custom to accompany the entrance of important characters with music. But these musical parts only became of importance when they were moved to the end of the act.

These *entr'actes,* called *intermedii,* were, in the beginning, purely instrumental. Their music is for the most part lost, but we possess instructions in the text books which give an adequate idea of the relation of the music to the drama.

But gradually the *intermedii* were enlarged to such an extent that Antonio Francesco Grazzini could write in 1582, ' Formerly the *intermedio* was an appendage of the comedy; nowadays the comedy is an appendage of the *intermedio*.'

Besides purely instrumental music, songs in madrigal form also made their appearance, linked together in such a way that it is possible to speak of a madrigal drama. The *Amfiparnasso* of Orazio Vecchi represents their highest achievement. From this it was a natural step to the monodic drama, as is evident when we consider that the desire for convincing characterization could not be satisfied for long with the expression of the feelings of an individual by a company of singers.

The second source, the liturgical drama with music led in the Middle Ages to Complaints of the Virgin and Passion Plays, which later gave way to the Italian *rappresentazione* of the sixteenth century in Florence and other towns of central Italy.

The true origin of the religious semi-dramatic form of the Oratorio, which appears about 1600, is to be found in the *Laudi* which already contained elements of dialogue. Through them it became possible to develop a religious art, independent of the liturgy, which finally led to the Oratorio. But this gradual development was cut short, and given a fixed form by the intervention of a circle of cultured amateurs who met, as has been said, towards the end of the sixteenth century, at the house of Count Bardi in Florence, to revive Greek tragedy.

Here, as in other spheres, the precepts of the Greek and

Roman writers were the point of departure for all discussion of art, and the decisions of Plato and Aristotle were of absolute authority to the Florentine *camerata*.

Starting from the knowledge that Greek tragedy was not spoken but sung, Count Bardi and his friends tried to call this lost dramatic style back to life. As has been said, the stage was well prepared, and the musicians of the circle, Caccini and Peri, were inspired by these discussions, whose importance they fully acknowledged, to a change of style, or, it would be better to say, to the consistent use of a style which already existed in embryo.

The real manifesto against the old style, the 'Declaration of War against Counterpoint,' as Ambros called it, came from the originator of the whole movement, Count Bardi. He wrote a long treatise, addressed to Caccini, on Greek music and the art of *bel canto*. As evidence of the effect of ancient music on the hearer he adduced a number of well-known myths and stories which he, the enlightened scholar, treats, surprisingly enough, as incontrovertible facts.

'But now-a-days,' he wrote, 'music falls into two main divisions; one belongs to counterpoint. The other should be called *arte di ben cantare.*' He criticizes the artificial style of the madrigal, and finds fault, for example, with the fact that the bass moves in sustained notes while the higher parts have a quicker movement. 'Our composers,' he says, 'would consider it a deadly sin if they happened to hear the voices at the same moment on the same syllable of the text and on notes of the same rhythmical value. The more they bring the parts into motion the more gifted they consider themselves. . . . And since we now find ourselves in such impenetrable darkness, we want at least to try to make a little light for poor Music, for, since her decline up to the present day she has not found, in so many centuries, one composer who thinks about her needs, who does not rather force her into the ways of her mortal enemy, Counterpoint.'

The most important means, he says, of improving music is to pay attention to the verse rhythm and not to imitate the musicians of the present day who, to flatter their own inclinations, destroy the verse and tear it to pieces. Thus, Bardi demands what Wagner was to call ' the birth of *melos* from the rhythm of speech.'

The first attempt in the recitative style was made by Vicenzo Galilei, the father of the famous astronomer. He had written a dialogue in the style of Plato on the old and new music. He had also discovered the ancient Greek hymn of Mesomedes, which was only deciphered in the nineteenth century. Yet this discovery seems to have given him a strong impulse to revive the lost art, and, if it could not be done by deciphering the document, to replace it by a fitting new composition. He therefore set to music the words of Count Ugolino in Dante's *Divina Commedia*. He himself sang the work, accompanied by several viols. This seems still to have been in the style of those madrigals already mentioned, in which a polyphonic work was so performed that only the highest part was sung. The novelty seems to have been the dramatic character of the recitative voice part.

The real development to drama, however, first occurred when Bardi had already left Florence, called to Rome by Pope Clement XIII. Now the circle met at the house of Jacopo Corsi. Here Peri took the lead. He was the pupil of Cristoforo Malvezzi, and had had a better training than his rival Caccini. His extraordinary virtuosity on the organ and the other keyboard instruments was of importance for the technique of his compositions. He also possessed a good soprano voice, which gave him the *entrée* to all the aristocratic salons of Florence. The Duke, too, had made him Director of Music, and he felt that this position placed him above all other musicians.

Besides Peri, Rinuccini the librettist must be mentioned as influential. He was the poet of most of the opera texts of the period, and he influenced their style for a full century. He too was filled with the idea of the supremacy of Greek tragedy, and he tried to realize this ideal, believing that through a well constructed plot, elevated diction, and concise expression, it provided an excellent basis for the musical setting.

Thus the prerequisites were established out of which the new form of the *dramma per musica* could develop.

iv

From what has been said it is clear that those who were contemporary with the change felt that they were faced with an evolution in music, not a sudden break with the past as was assumed in the early days of the study of the history of music, even if some composers had no small opinion of the part they played in the movement. The numerous treatises and opera-prologues which contain the programme of the new movement prove this. In most of the treatises we can see the effort of the musicians to compare the old with the new and to bring into prominence one or the other, according to the party to which they belong. In most cases, of course, the treatises end with the praises of the New Art. It is not clear who was pre-eminent in the development of the monodic style to real recitative. Three men were cited in the various treatises as *Inventori* : Giulio Caccini, Jacopo Peri, and Marco da Gagliano. Nowadays it is generally agreed that the true pioneer of the modern movement was Don Carlo Gesualdo, Principe di Venosa, whose vocal style, in his madrigals, had shown the way to his successors. It is, too, a most remarkable fact that his madrigals survived through several editions, an unusual circumstance and a sign that they must have been eagerly studied by musicians.

In the treatise *Discorsi e Regole sovra la musica* of Severo Bonini the privilege of discovering the new style is attributed to Giulio Caccini detto Romano alone, and Jacopo Peri and Marco da Gagliano are only mentioned in the second place. But the author relies mainly for his account on Caccini's own Preface to the *Nuove Musiche*, since the *Discorsi* is concerned with the same subject.

Marco da Gagliano, on the other hand, in the preface to

his opera *Dafne* gives another version of the facts and brings forward Jacopo Peri as the discoverer of the new style : ' It was Jacopo Peri who discovered that ingenious manner of speech-song which the whole of Italy admires. I shall never be weary of praising him, since everyone must praise him unceasingly, and every music-lover has the songs from the *Orfeo* constantly before him. But I must also say that no one can fully appreciate the beauty and power of his songs who has not heard them performed by him.'

Caccini, a most self-conscious artist, speaks specifically of his own merits in the preface to the *Nuove Musiche,* which was Bonini's main source. Certain expressions from this preface have gained general currency and form the kernel of most accounts of the origins of monody. It is therefore necessary to point out that Caccini's statements need to be treated with caution. The beginning of the preface shows Caccini's opinion of himself : ' If I have finished my studies in the art of singing with the famous Scipione del Palla, my teacher, and have not published my madrigals and arias, written over a period of years, it is because I did not think them worth publication, and believed that they had met with honour enough, and even beyond their deserts, when I knew my music to be continually performed by the most famous singers of Italy and by the most distinguished amateurs.'

Caccini's modest opening is, it is clear, only a rhetorical trick to throw into stronger contrast the wide circulation of his music. Of great importance, however, is his emphatic insistence on ' a certain noble subordination of singing ' (*una certa nobile sprezzatura del canto*), for music ' should be speech and rhythm in the first place, sound only in the second, and not the other way round.' This is the central point of his teaching, and it is in conformity with Gluck's remark, that when he began to compose he tried to forget that he was a musician.

Caccini demanded of the singer a perfect understanding of the sense and the emotional content of what he sang. It was not enough merely to have behind one a long experience of singing. One must also, by virtue of intelligence, be able to master the whole material. ' This talent,' he says, ' is incompatible with any half-measures, and the more brilliant characteristics are contained in it, the greater effort and care must the teacher expend, industriously and lovingly to draw them out.'

As has already been said, the battle against counterpoint was a central part of the movement. Counterpoint was regarded as the principal evil, because it had become associated with repetition and lengthening of the text to the destruction of the sense. Its opponents set themselves against the *Laceramento della Poesia* and opposed the idea that in the madrigal different words should be sung at the same time. This revolt against the ruling tendency is to be explained as the reaction of the Italians against the complicated contrapuntal style of the Netherlands, which was practised in Venice. In the sixteenth century famous Northern masters had been brought there as teachers, but their art, apparently, never became really popular. It was too foreign to the Italian character in feeling and technique for it ever to mean to them more than a temporary excursion into a strange world.

But now the revolt against counterpoint was reinforced by a style of composition which originated in Spain and spread over South Italy. With its clearly organized simple structure of chords it soon gained a large following. That it was due to Spanish influence was not known until the most recent period of research. It was only when interest was aroused in Spanish vocal music that problems which had seemed obscure and insoluble took on a new aspect.

Through Spain and Italy the East made its last bid to influence the West, and even if it could no longer offer the plenitude of those times when an unbroken stream of caravans from the great metropolises of Asia made their way to the coasts of the Mediterranean bringing gifts and treasure to the West, when monks, artists, and craftsmen from Persia, Armenia, and Syria brought their native culture to the ports of Italy and France, and workmen and musicians penetrated as far as the Rhine, yet even this last effort of a culture which was continually losing ground before the increasing power of the West, must be accounted of great importance. It is the last wave in the great backwards and forwards ebb which was responsible for the whole relationship of the Greeks and the Persians, ending, with the temporary victory of the Greeks, in Hellenism, against which a proportionately violent reaction from the East set in.

The Spaniards used the favourite instrument of the Arabs, the lute, and a considerable literature arose for voice and lute accompaniment. The fact that the instrument was so well adapted to play chords sharpened the Spanish ear for harmony.

In the few pieces of music which survive, a strong feeling for harmonic progressions is evident and a concentration on the highest part at a time when, in Italy, the *cantus* was still in the middle part. One document proves that the importance of the highest part was already appreciated: the prohibition in the *Libro primo de la declaracion de instrumentos musicales* by Juan Bermudo (1549) of the introduction of melodic ornament by the performers where it is not expressly required by the composer. This prohibition of the weakening of the melodic line means that a very strong feeling existed for developed *cantilena,* complete in itself and needing no ornament.

Caccini's complaint of the singers who ignore his instructions and make an abuse of ornament corresponds to the prohibition of Juan Bermudo, and indeed, if we examine the works of the Italian theorists on the art of singing we shall be struck by the excessive richness of the art of ornamentation in the second half of the sixteenth century.

The Florentine Reformers did not, however, as is always assumed, abolish ornament: they systematized it. They themselves wrote very important ornaments. In the new style for solo voice accompanied by the *basso continuo,* on the other hand, the ornaments could no longer cause such confusion.

Caccini occupied the most extreme position among the

theorists. He considered that passages were only the invention of those who did not know how to express real emotion. If one was capable of this, he said, passages would without doubt be cast aside, for nothing could be in greater opposition to truth than they are. He himself only used them at tranquil moments, and in final cadences. This new style, therefore (and it must be strongly stressed), was not concerned with recitative singing in the sense in which Monteverdi developed it in his late operas, but with expressive solo singing. The innovation was the complete predominance of the highest part, and, in order to carry through this principle, the whole art and achievement of polyphonic singing was sacrificed. Even though there was a last flowering of the madrigal in the seventeenth century it was only important for its harmonic subtleties, not for the art of its polyphony.

The means by which the new style was systematically developed was, as has been said, the introduction of the figured bass. It is evident that the result of this was to make the performer concentrate on correct, and later on interesting harmonies rather than on a beautiful and smooth progression of parts. A feeling for harmonic sequences, for intensification and relaxation in the harmony, for extension of cadences was however also developed. The aim was always to develop these even further, increasingly to expand the melodic curve and to group the chords within this curve with ever increasing effectiveness.

Two other harmonic processes mark the beginning of monody : the loss of chromatics, and the introduction of freely placed dissonances.

In the last years of the sixteenth century chromaticism had developed to an extraordinary degree of subtlety. But with the end of polyphonic vocal music it became restricted mainly to the upper part, and one of the most important methods of composition, chromaticism in the middle part, was gradually lost through the uncertainty of the notation. But even in the highest and lowest parts it gradually vanished during the course of the seventeenth century and was maintained only in a few cases. It still played a very important part in a few standard *bassi ostinati* until late in the eighteenth century.

The process of freeing dissonance began with the introduction of the unprepared dominant seventh chord. It was this which helped to build up our modern cadence. This tendency to use the dominant structure is older than is generally assumed. Even in the most flourishing period of the church modes a similar effect was attempted with the chord of the fifth. But the systematic fixing of the cadences by means of the dominant seventh chord and the decrease in importance of all the intervals before the fifth which took place from the seventeenth century onwards, was new. The freeing of dissonance from the rules of counterpoint, its use according to the impulse of the composer is, again, a sign of awakening subjectivity.

Monteverdi dared to introduce an unprepared ninth followed by an equally unprepared seventh and to make the resolution only after these chords. This was, for the period, an unheard-of boldness and it called forth opposition. A theorist, the Canon Giovanni Maria Artusi of Bologna opposed such harmonic freedoms in a work which appeared in 1600, *L'Artusi overo delle imperfezione della moderna musica*. He maintained that these madrigals were aberrations and would lead to barbarism. People tried to excuse violations of the rules as the ' new style ' but it was not practicable to overthrow the soundly based rules of the theorists. ' The new composers only want to satisfy the ear and to deceive it through the rapidity of the movement. But they forget that their cantilenas must also be judged by the understanding. They are ignoramuses who only want to make a noise and do not know what one ought to write and what one ought not.'

Here the academic line of argument is easily recognizable. Since Monteverdi did not write in accordance with the rules of the classical theorists, his music, even if it sounds well, is to be blamed. Monteverdi defended himself from this criticism. He accused Artusi of only judging the notes without the text, which, alone, could reveal the meaning of his work. Here we

find once more Caccini's demand that the music must adapt
itself to the sense of the words.

The conflict between music and words has never ceased
from this time onwards and in periods of the predominance
of music over words it has led to the great reforms which
are associated with the names of Gluck and Wagner.

v

If we take together all these features which mark the new
style in contrast to earlier music—predominance of a highest
part with coloratura used for sound painting and declamation
following the sense of the text with reduced importance of all
other parts in contrast to the highest, which tries to unite and
render in itself the content of all the parts; the beginning of
a harmonic logic, a careful consideration of the harmonic
structure and, in connection with this, the gradual freeing of
dissonance; the beginning of a characteristic instrumental
style utilizing the special qualities of the instruments to enliven
the melody as such (orchestral colour), the growth of new
forms whose development continues up to the present day and
whose chief characteristics can be regarded as thematic structure, using a crescendo based on the repetition of a motive—
then all these features, which are paralleled in the other arts,
point to the desire for personal expression, for larger proportions, greater emotional range, a necessity to give expression
to every emotion. If for example we make a brief comparison
with architecture it is clear that the ambition of the Baroque
architect to bring together all parts in a self-contained whole
in order to achieve an impression of completeness corresponds
to the form of an ever bolder melodic curve. Just as in architecture in order to achieve this end by visual means the centre
of the façade was emphasized and certain parts of the wall
brought forward from it while the parts at the side were
pushed back, so in music an attempt was made to concentrate
on a few important points by an enhanced harmonic structure
at the climaxes. Just as those parts of the façade which are to

be focal points are emphasized by doors with elaborate portals, by pillars or windows with ornamented pediments, so those parts of a musical composition which are to be emphasized are brought out by the scoring. In architecture great use is made of optical illusion brought about by the intensification of shadow. Corresponding to this, Baroque music developed to an increasing degree the contrast between *piano* and *forte*, *solo* and *tutti*. The architects favoured pillars placed in a flat surface and intended to give the impression of support, though they are built in such a way that their only use is to break up the surface. In music middle parts began to be written which simulate a contrapuntal movement while in reality they fulfil a definite rhythmical function. As Baroque architecture tries to break through or to dissolve a closed line, for example in the breaking up of the contour of the gable, the interruption of the cornice by jutting moulding, backward or forward projections which throw shadows, the modification of the outline with ornament, so in music the corresponding tendency is to be found to keep the melodic line as much in motion as possible, to ornament it with more sustained notes and to introduce coloratura at important points. To the splendour of the late Baroque façades, the richly gilded interiors of churches, corresponds in music the growth of orchestral colour, the conscious use of single instruments or groups of instruments to capture the listener by the charm of the sound. Just as the interiors of many churches seem not to be covered by a solid roof but, through the painter's continuation of the architect's work, to extend into the open space of heaven, filled with troops of angels and with clouds, so in music a similar feeling of boundless space is produced when in a Mass several vocal and instrumental choirs of different range seem to sound from a mysterious distance. In music the association of certain ideas with corresponding sounds was so highly developed that the emotional content of the music can be determined from the use of the instruments. Tone-symbols arose which form the basis of the modern art of scoring.

The first period of Baroque music, the period of conflict

and of the first creations, lasted up to the middle of the
seventeenth century, up to the time when the architectonic
forms of opera, oratorio, and cantata, fluid to begin with,
hardened into rigid formulae. Now emotion becomes conventional, the fresh dramatic impulse weakened to a
sentimental lyricism.

The music drama has outgrown its youth and entered on
its period of maturity. From now on dramatic proportion
between words and music is at an end. The aria becomes predominant—from the musical point of view an event of the
greatest importance since almost all problems of form were
solved by the tripartite form of the aria, but from the point of
view of the text, it meant the end of a truly dramatic plot.
For, to provide for the lyrical development of the aria the
whole action was forced into *recitativo secco* which became
musically less and less important. This state of affairs only
ended when a reforming movement set in with the same
principles and archaizing tendencies as the Florentines had
had, and was given form and expression by Gluck.

But instrumental music had already, at an earlier period,
developed in an increasingly elaborate way, and it finally
became an important factor at the moment when the symphony of the opera, separated from the music drama, was
performed in the concert hall, and when true symphonies
were composed without any connection with an opera. These
concert symphonies were most common in Austria and South
Germany, and they are the first sign of emancipation from
the Italian taste. A fourth movement, the minuet, was added
to the usual three and thus the form was reached in which
Haydn, Mozart, and Beethoven expressed their most profound
feelings and ideas, and which, up to the present day, even if
in an altered and extended form, remains the most important
medium of musical expression.

II

The Beginnings of Opera in Vienna

G REAT AS WAS the interest which the Viennese Court
took in the music-drama which flourished in Italy at the
beginning of the seventeenth century, the institution of a permanent opera was prevented by a continual state of war until
the accession of Leopold I in 1658. But it is important to
notice that attempts had already been made under the influence of Ferdinand III, himself an enthusiastic musician and
the composer of an astonishing number of works, to accli-
matize the new form in his Empire.

A beginning was made with short cantatas and semi-
dramatic scenes in the popular form of introductions to the
ballets which were usually danced by the Court at festivities.
A *melodramma, Allegrezze del mondo,* was performed for the
marriage of Ferdinand III to the Infanta Maria Anna of
Spain in 1631, and at the same celebrations a *canzone, Orfeo,*
formed the introduction to a ballet in which the Archduchess
Claudia appeared as the Moon, and the ladies of the Court
as planets. At the coronation of Ferdinand on December 30th,
1636, a ballet was performed, preceded by a poem of
homage, *Vaticinio di Silvano,* a pastoral by Valeriano Bon-
vicino. The lands of the Empire appear on a triumphal car
and sing a chorus glorifying the festivity. Then they dismount
from the car and render their homage, first together and
then separately. The prototypes of this allegorical scene can
be traced far back. Such acts of homage are the subject of
most of the *intermedii* of the sixteenth century. Later, too,
they remained very popular. It is only necessary to recall

c

that in the famous festival opera of Cesti, *Il pomo d'oro,* the
appearance of the lands of the Empire is worked into the
action of the drama.

A few years later, on the birthday of the Empress Maria
Anna a real *dramma per musica* was performed, *Ariadna
abbandonata da Theseo e sposata dal Dio Baccho, nell' giorno
felicissimo della nascità Dell' Augustissima Imperatrice Maria
Infanta di Spagna, etc. Rappresentata da Musici Cesarei,
Composta dal Conte Francesco Bonacossi, Coppiero di Sua
Maestà Cesarea.* Unfortunately only the text, not the music,
is preserved.

The parasite, Zan Tripu, introduces himself with an eating
song :

> *Satiar le brame*
> *Della mia fame*
> *Gia mai non spero*
> *Ancor che un Bue io mi mangiassi intiero.*
>
> *Ogni gran pesce*
> *Che nel mar oresco*
> *Non più in palato*
> *Satisfar tanto, che io non sia affamato.*
>
> *Un grosso Armento*
> *Cent'ova e cento*
> *Pan sperarei*
> *Di poter divorar co denti miei.*
>
> *O che gran rabbia*
> *Il cor' arrabia*
> *Ben in un di*
> *Mangiare chi mi fè, chi mi nutri.*

One seems to recognize the parasite Ergasilus from the
Captivi of Plautus who (Act IV, scene iii) is ready to work
havoc in the dining-room. This figure will be encountered

again and again in the course of the next few years, in the texts of the Viennese opera.

Then the Pedant enters and addresses a speech to the Parasite, which the latter fails to understand, because of the numerous latinisms which the Pedant employs. The Pedant wants to improve him, but the Parasite only looks for improvement in the kitchen. But the punishment of his greed is not slow in coming. In the second act he sets to work on a dish which suddenly begins to grow, and gets bigger and bigger. Terrified, he sees in this a delusion of the devil, and runs away, crying:

O che miro? perche cresce,
E s' inalza le vivanda! ohimè;
Zan Tripù che sara?
Ahi chi aiuto mi da?
Soccorso ohimè, soccorso à un sfortunato,
Che il Diavolo nel piatto hà ritrovato.

Similar *buffo* scenes are to be found in the text of the opera *Armida e Rinaldo* which was also performed in 1641, and which treats the Armida story in a pastoral background; that is to say, the main action is only a pretext for the introduction of sirens and satyrs, who reflect the cheerful, joyous aspect of things.

A satyr thus sings his avowal of an Anacreontic view of the world:

Io non sprezzo il buon licore
Del gran Baccho, ma il Dio Amore
È il mio ben, è il mia gioia,
Ma però quel non m' annoia;
Sempre mai il tuo gran Dio
Rispettai ma non tu il mio.

The same lighthearted, sensuous joy in life is expressed in the seductive song of two noble maidens who wish to charm the knights Ubaldo and Carlo:

Deh fermate o Cavallieri
Vostro piè troppo fugace.
Questo è il regno de' i piaceri,
Qui si gode eterna pace,
Cio che alli avidi volessi,
Piu diletta, e che piu piace
Qui vedrete, e senza noie
Bearete immense gioie.

Here, as in the works mentioned before, the chorus had an important part to play. Festive processions and *canzonetti* of the type usually sung with ballets occupied much space. Two years later, however, in 1643, an opera was performed which must have seemed revolutionary : the *Egisto* of Cavalli.

Francesco Cavalli is one of the greatest figures in the history of opera. He had the good fortune to live at the beginning of an epoch, after the way had been pointed out to him by Monteverdi. Together with Cesti he brought the most brilliant period of the Venetian opera to perfection. It is no mere chance that the first music-drama of real importance that we encounter in the history of the Viennese opera comes from a Venetian. A close relationship existed between the cultural life of the two cities. In Vienna, as in Venice, the same mixture is to be found of seriousness and charming gaiety, distinct from the Neapolitan frivolity, and the French gravity. It is true that the art of Venice, like that of Vienna, underwent from time to time a strong influence from France. This, however, never remains as a foreign element, but is immediately transformed and naturalized.

Cavalli is the Wagner of the seventeenth century. He began with choral operas with texts by a great dramatist, Francesco Busenello, and went on to solo-opera, the first of which was *L'Egisto Rè di Cipro.*

The form of solo-opera created something of universal appeal out of what was, in the highest sense of the word, occasional. It owes its existence to the conditions of the Venetian theatre. Here a rich bourgoisie had come into power.

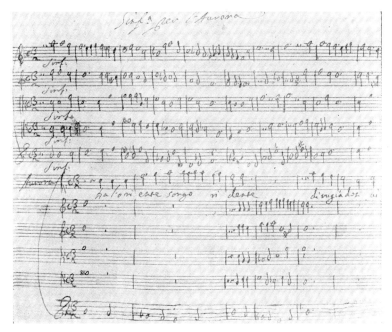

Page from Cavalli's autographed
score of *L'Egisto*

(*By permission of J. M. Dent & Sons Ltd.*)

Easily obtained wealth, the result of the unique position of Venice in world trade, favoured the development of art. The varigated population of nobles, townspeople and foreign travellers, seafarers and adventurers lived, once the dark period of tyrannic government was over, in a perpetual festival. And it was above all the new form of music-drama which was the centre of interest. As early as 1640 there were three opera-houses: S. Cassiano, SS. Giovanni e Paolo and S. Moisè. Later the Teatro novissimo was added, but it was destroyed in 1647 and replaced by the Teatro SS. Apostoli, so that from 1650 onwards there were four permanent stages. Thus, while up to this point opera had chiefly served to provide a background for festivities at the courts of Princes, it now became, through the Venetian practice, popular for the first time, and developed to the important cultural factor which it has remained up to the present day.

Monteverdi, whose *Orfeo*, important though it is, is erroneously regarded as initiating a new stylistic tendency, created in his magnificent last work, the *Incoronazione di Poppea*, a new, highly personal means of expression. From the point of view of music drama it was of the greatest importance that the chorus was already pushed well into the background, so that it meant only a step further for Cavalli to eliminate it even to the conventional calls, like ' *all' armi*,' which could easily be sung by supernumeraries.

The theatres of Venice were only held on lease by managers. They could not afford the luxury of an elaborate production, a big orchestra and a chorus. The main responsibility, therefore, fell to the musician, who had to achieve the most intensely dramatic effect possible.

It is not difficult to understand how important the performance of *Egisto* must have been for Vienna; how novel the terse passionate dialogue must have seemed. If the political disturbances of the time had not hindered every activity of opera, it would be hard to say how far the music drama would have developed in Vienna. In fact, however, only a few occasional cantatas were produced, and, in 1648, for the

marriage of Ferdinand III to the Archduchess Maria Leo-
poldina of Innsbruck, in Pressburg, a *dramma imperfetta,
I Trionfi d'Amore.*

In the Prologue of this opera Venus and Cupid enter.
Venus asks him to show the world his power, so as to prove
himself the stronger before Diana and Pallas. Cupid accordingly visits Vulcan to get new arrows for his quiver, in order
to begin his game with mankind. The figure of Vulcan is
presented in an unconventional way. He expresses pity for
mankind, who only serve the gods as the instruments of their
caprices:

> *Il misero mortal è fatto in terra*
> *Gioco e scherzo de Dei*
> *Ed à ludibrio suo convien che soffre*
> *Rappresentar qua giu varie sembianze.*

And now, with the second act, the real action begins, the
story of Odysseus on the island of Circe. It is, again, enliv-
ened by a pastoral sub-plot, which provides an opportunity
for hunting choruses.

Cupid, with his arrows, enflames all the characters with
love. Even the old negress Cosmea cannot protect herself
from him, and falls in love with Odysseus, whom she tries to
convince of the charms of her dusky complexion. But he
gives her to understand that, while he acknowledges her
beauty, he has no enthusiasm for black. He turns to Circe,
to whom he declares his love. Together they both sing a
melancholy love-duet which, like much in this drama rises
above the usual level of court poetry.

> *Godiamo, che il tempo e breve*
> *Ne mancano i malori*
> *Cade e fiocca la neve*
> *Dove risero i fiori.*

But Cosmea too finds a lover to suit her in Arcigalante.

In the fifth act the pastoral plot once more comes to the

fore, and the work ends with the avowal of the power of Cupid who appears with Venus in the *Licenza* and pays homage to the imperial pair.

After the conclusion of the Westphalian Peace a gradual increase in performances of music-drama at the Viennese Court can be observed.

The Emperor Ferdinand III himself composed a *Dramma musicum,* and a second opera by Cavalli, the famous *Giasone,* was also performed in Vienna. For the marriage of Philip IV to the Archduchess Marianna in Brussels, Giuseppe Zamboni composed *Ulisse errante nell' isolo di Circe.* The score is adorned with magnificent aquarelles of the stage sets. At the Diet of Regensburg in 1653 the Emperor was accompanied by sixty musicians and caused a theatre to be built, at great cost, and the opera *L'inganno d'amore,* by his Kapellmeister Antonio Bastali, to be performed.

Under the Emperor Leopold I, Vienna became a centre for contemporary opera. Immediately after his succession to the throne an increase can be observed in the number of operas performed, which goes on from year to year. Leopold was originally intended for a learned and devout calling and had an excellent teacher of music in Wolfgang Ebner. His own talents, according to the testimony of Marshal Grammont, who saw him in 1658 at his coronation in Frankfurt, were for the composition of sad melodies. But the Marshal was exaggerating when he said that the Emperor's only pleasure was in such compositions, for he loved every kind of music and wrote informally to Count Poettig at a time when the court was in mourning: ' This carnival I ought to have kept quiet on account of the mourning, but we had several little entertainments *in camera,* for it doesn't help the dead if one is sad.' Leopold had a special predilection for Italian music and singing, but to please his wife, Margareta Theresia, he also used the Spanish language, and himself set to music Spanish *entremeses* and commissioned his Ambassador Count Poettig to send him compositions from Spain, because his wife longed for the music of her native land. He

knew how to attract important singers and instrumentalists to
his court; he took musicians with him when he travelled; it
was he who made Vienna a centre of musical life.

In this period an entirely original type of Italian opera was
developed which produced works of strong individuality in
spite of their connection with court ceremonial, like the
Orontea of the male soprano Vismarri which was performed
in 1660. This opera has a dramatic verve, a pregnancy of
melodic expression which recalls Cavalli and deserves the
highest praise.

The conservative tendency was represented by the composers Felice Sances and Antonio Bertali. Besides them Pietro
Andrea was active. Draghi, too, the most prolific musician at
the court of Leopold I, began his career as a librettist, but
later became a composer. The most important figure, however,
is Marc' Antonio Cesti who, after the success of his *Dori,* was
summoned to Vienna and commissioned to write the festival
opera for the marriage celebrations of Leopold I and Margareta Theresia. This work was to be performed among a
host of other events in honour of the arrival of the imperial
bride from Spain, though in fact, through various delays, the
performance took place later. It represents the most perfect
type of the early Baroque festival opera.

' This time,' wrote the librettist Francesco Sbarra, ' I would
rather have you as a spectator than as a reader of the work
I am submitting to you.' It would be impossible, he went on,
to give any idea in words of the excellence of the music, the
splendour of the spectacles, the magnificence of the scenery,
the richness of the costumes, the variety of the dances, the
daring of the combats, the military exactness of the siege and
defence of the stronghold, together with other miracles of
art. But one could feel convinced that this festival performance
would exceed everything seen up to the present in splendour
and magnificence.

Even before the arrival of the imperial bride a ballet was
performed to celebrate the event. The music was written by
the ballet-composer of the Viennese court, Johann Heinrich

Schmelzer. It was the *Concorso dell' allegrezza universale.*
The text was written in Italian, German and Spanish. The
ballet began with a chorus of singers who performed a
canzonetta. Then four cavaliers appeared, assembled from all
parts of Europe, from the Manzanares, from the Tiber, from
the Seine, and from the Rhine, in order to pay their homage.
In the second dance they are accompanied by envoys from
Africa, Asia and the New World. The entrance of two
gardeners who set up nine-pins provides a gay *intermezzo* and
interrupts the ceremonious figures.

The dances which follow after ' the Kingdom and the lands
of the Empire ' have entreated heaven for an heir to the
throne, are also gay in character. Three Satyrs display their
skill. Mercury appears and three *Amoretti* dance a round. A
French cavalier enters with his lady. An envoy from Holland
and two old women are anxious not to be left behindhand,
and so is ' the merry Scaramuccia.' Then a Spanish cavalier
and his lady comes, and they all unite in a final ballet which
the chorus of singers accompanies with a *canzonetta* in
renewed glorification of the bridal pair.

This ballet can be regarded as the prelude to the festivities.
It is easy to recognize the forerunners of this genre in the
usual Italian court ballets, which were performed in Vienna,
and which remained in use up to the eighteenth century.

Much more important, however, was the *Balletto a cavallo*
(*La Contesa dell' Aria e dell' Acqua,* text by Francesco
Sbarra) which was the central part of the festivities, and which
the Emperor Leopold had prepared for his bride. It had been
assumed that the Infanta would arrive in mid-summer, and
all preparations were made accordingly. But just before her
journey was due to begin she fell ill with a fever, and messen-
gers had to be sent to carry the news to the Emperor. After
her recovery she was brought by a splendidly equipped ship,
La Reale di Spagna, escorted by a Spanish flotilla, to Finale,
where the Imperial General Count Montecuccoli awaited her.
From there her journey to Vienna lasted three months. The
Emperor, whom etiquette forbade to escort his bride in person,

sent messenger after messenger to meet her. In Trent she was
greeted by Cardinal Count Harrach, in Villach by Count
Weissenwolf, in Styria by Count Wolkenstein, at the
Austrian frontier by Obersthofmarschall Count Starhemberg.
When she passed through Graz she was received with an
Ossequioso applauso by Marc' Antonio Rossini, Canon in
Brünn. The Emperor came to meet her at Schott-Wien,
impatient to see his bride, whom he only knew from portraits
and the descriptions of his courtiers. After a short meeting he
left her and returned to Vienna to prepare for the official
reception. In spite of the wintry season the plan of performing the ' Equestrian ballet ' in the open air was not abandoned.

From the aesthetic point of view, however, Cesti's festival
opera, *Il pomo d'oro*,[1] is of far greater importance than this
show-piece. Its text, too, was by Sbarra. Besides the poet and
the composer, however, the brilliant architect Ludovico
Burnacini was responsible for a large share of the work,
designing the décors and machines, which were extraordinarily magnificent and costly even for the period.

The framework of Baroque opera was fixed for the next
half-century in Vienna by the *Pomo d'oro*. It was impossible
to produce anything more spectacular. It only remained to
develop details. The genres of instrumental pieces and aria
were enlarged and elaborated and more and more stress was
laid on the skilful exploitation of a richly ornamental singing
voice. This meant the abandonment of the principles which
had called the *dramma per musica* into being, and the subordination of opera to the requirements of the court, of
oratorio to those of the Church. This resulted in a transformation which is to be understood chiefly in terms of social
history. The dramatic music which in Italy was to an increasing extent written for the rising class of the bourgoisie,
remained in Vienna an art of the court and was therefore
more conservative in attitude, more solid and monumental
in structure. The most recent developments of music in Italy

[1] A full analysis of *Il pomo d'oro* will be found in ' A Festival Opera
of the Seventeenth Century ' in the present volume, p. 55f.

were well known, but the old forms were carefully preserved. Even when Neapolitan light opera made its way, after 1700, to Vienna—it is true through the medium of Venice—the grand style of the festival opera was maintained, and experienced a second spring through Johann Josef Fux, especially in his opera *Costanza e Fortezza* written for the coronation of Charles VI as King of Bohemia in 1723.

The performance took place on August 28th, the birthday of the Empress, at the Hradschin, the Royal residence, in Prague. On this occasion, too, the opera was only a part of the festivities. Rehearsals were held throughout July and August and the Empress attended one of the last, on August 23rd. Foreigners flocked to the town, partly to attend the coronation celebrations, partly to see the opera. Among them was J. J. Quantz the famous flautist, the teacher of Frederick the Great. He wrote a graphic account of the opera. A hundred singers and two hundred instrumentalists took part. The cost of the performance amounted, according to Apostolo Zeno, to 50,000 gulden, for a theatre was specially built for the occasion. 'The music,' reported Quantz, 'was by the Imperial Kapellmeister, the famous old Fux. It was more suited to the church than to the theatre, but nevertheless it was very magnificent.' The string-writing, he went on to say, in the *ritornelli*, though it might often seem stiff and dry on paper, gave a very good impression on such a scale and with so many players. A better impression, indeed, than a fashionable piece of music, decked out with numerous small notes would have done in this instance. The many choruses of the Prague opera were used, in the French manner, for the ballets as well. The scenes were all brilliantly illuminated. Because of the number of the performers, the Imperial Kapellmeister, Caldara, gave the beat. The old Fux himself whom, since he was afflicted with the gout, the Emperor had caused to be brought in a litter from Vienna to Prague, had the pleasure of listening, from a seat not far from the Emperor's, to this extraordinarily magnificent performance of his work.

The theatre specially built for this performance was

designed by Giuseppe Galli-Bibbiena, who had shortly before been appointed chief theatre architect in place of his father, now almost blind. Deriving from the School of Albani he developed a light, gaily colourful style of architecture quite different from the powerful greatness of a Fischer von Erlach. This style is to be seen in a series of palaces and churches of the period. Its aim is the complete subordination of the plastic to the values of painting. Surface and line are dissolved in colour and light. The painted walls give an illusion of greater depth, the painted ceiling of extension into endless space.

Giuseppe Galli-Bibbiena, who worked first in Mailand and then in Barcelona, had already shown his powers in the settings for Fux's *Angelica* in 1716. A remarkable letter is preserved from Lady Montague to Pope describing this performance. In the décors of *Costanza e Fortezza* he made the most dazzling use of his art and designed the most elaborate settings, using machines on which living tableaux could be presented, and costumes which were extravagantly adorned with jewels.

Fux's music is, in the arias and recitatives, often conventional and to present-day taste of wearisome length. But this is the case in all operas of the time, which clearly bear the marks of a transition period. On the other hand, there are moments of real genius and greatness which rise above the conventions of the age. Such moments are not lacking in Fux's other operas, nor in those of his contemporaries, Conti and Caldara, proving that even late Baroque opera could achieve a high level, and demonstrating the continuity of the brilliant tradition whose first great landmark was the *Pomo d'oro*.

Even Gluck paid tribute to this tradition when in 1751 he set to music *L'Eroe Cinese* by Metastasio for an entertainment which Prince Joseph Frederick of Sachsen-Hildburghausen gave for the Empress Maria Theresa at Schlosshof, though it is true that this little work will not bear comparison with the magnificent conceptions of Baroque grand opera.

The times had changed. Foreign ideas had begun to work; a new epoch was preparing.

Once more music drama tried to attain to the ideals to which it owed its origin. Again, it turned to classical tragedy for a model. As a result opera entered on a phase of reaction against the stylization of the Baroque period and cultivated a realism which, starting with Gluck, led, by way of romantic opera, to Richard Wagner.

Yet Baroque left clear traces on the reformed opera. The fact of a tradition extending over a century could not be completely obliterated by the new direction of ideas. And it can repeatedly be observed how the characteristics of Baroque come to the surface, and then vanish again until a new wave leads to renewed stylization and to another era in which the Baroque ideal is influential in dramatic music.

III

Italian Musicians at the Austrian Court

ONE OF THE most significant changes known to the history of Western music occurred in the second half of the sixteenth century. At that time vocal polyphony, in the form of the madrigal for four or five voices, had reached its highest development. The boldness of the part-writing and the abundance of entirely new harmonic progressions seemed to offer unlimited possibilities. Two new elements acquired at this period a new importance, opening to music unexpected horizons. One was the predominance of a single voice over the others in the texture of a composition, the other was the new development of instrumental music. It is to this change, which came from Italy, that I refer. It reached its complete development at the opening of the seventeenth century, and to it the world owes the birth of two new forms of composition—opera and symphony.

At the junction of the sixteenth and seventeenth centuries Austria possessed three great centres of music at the courts of Vienna, Graz, and Innsbruck. Up to 1600 the musicians appointed to the royal court at Vienna and to the two archiducal courts were principally German and Dutch, partly French and Spanish; Italians were extremely rare. It was accepted as a matter of course that the director of the orchestra had to be Dutch. But as early as the reigns of the Emperors Maximilian II (1564-76) and Rudolph II (1576-1612) the directors of the court orchestra—Philippe de Monte and Jacques Regnard—were, so to speak, Italianized; and after the death of de Monte the reign of Italian music begins, which lasted for more than a hundred years without interruption. The first enthusiast for Italian music was Maximilian's brother, the Archduke Charles, resident at Graz. He engaged Italian trumpeters for his orchestra. He also admitted to his service Lodovico Zacconi, singer, composer and theorist, who dedicated to his noble patron the first part of his *Prattica di Musica* (1592). The Archduke's interest in his orchestra and the trouble he took to see that it was composed of outstanding musicians can be clearly seen from a report made by the Venetian ambassador, Michieli, where we find the following words: 'Ha una capella, e per quantità e per qualità dei musici che senza dubbio eccede quella di ogni altro principe.' The Archduke had harpsichords and string instruments sent from Italy. For wind instruments he relied chiefly on Vienna and Nuremberg, but these too came in part from Italy. His son Ferdinand, later Emperor, was passionately fond of music; he had a marked affection for the great Italian masters. He was a great admirer of Giovanni Gabrieli, Orazio Vecchi and Claudio Monteverdi. The period 1596-1619, when he was in residence at Graz, was a particularly brilliant epoch in the life of the town. After his coronation as Ferdinand II he transferred his orchestra to Vienna. His musicians were added to those of the Vienna court orchestra, bringing the total number up to more than eighty.

The outbreak of the Thirty Years' War was responsible for a diminution of interest in music at the court. This is the only reason we can give to explain the fact that none of the new music dramas was performed in the capital. It is not until the wedding of Ferdinand's son, later Ferdinand III, in 1631, that we find a *melodramma* with ballet—Prospero Bonarelli's *Allegrezze del Mondo*—performed at the Viennese court. With the accession of Ferdinand III in 1637 began the 'Golden Age' of music in Austria, characterized by the predominance of Vienna, whose glory eclipsed that of Graz and Innsbruck. Ferdinand was the first of the line of emperors who practised composition. The line came to an end with Charles VI in 1740.

This period is generally described as the epoch of Austrian Baroque. When it began, and indeed until 1700, it was principally Italian musicians and composers who imposed their own peculiar style on the Austrian court. From 1700 onwards we find an increase in the number and importance of Austrian musicians and composers, generally natives of Vienna. The fusion of the definitely Italian feeling for form with the Austrian sense of melody had the happy result of creating the style of the pre-classical Viennese composers. This style helped materially to prepare for the arrival of the glorious epoch of Austrian music associated with the names of Gluck, Haydn, Mozart, Beethoven, and Schubert—what may be called the Viennese classical period. The development of the manufacture of violins by the Italian master-craftsmen, the increased importance of string instruments in the orchestral ensemble and the perfecting of the technique of playing and of writing for violin and 'cello—all this had only a slight influence on the concert music written in Vienna; but it can be observed in the more extended use of string instruments in the symphonies, ritornelli, and arias of operas and oratorios. During the whole of this period Austrian music developed, from the aesthetic point of view, by maintaining close contact with the artistic principles which were established in Italy about 1600. The chief object of interest was music drama, oratorio, the cantata, and the Mass for chorus and orchestra. The preference given to pure *a cappella* music began to disappear; the feeling for orchestral sonority awoke and with it the taste for the sweet but full sound of string instruments. There came into being a style of writing specially designed for these instruments, and particularly for the violin.

The first great composer we meet in studying the history of opera at Vienna is Claudio Monteverdi with his *Il ritorno d'Ulisse in patria*. He is followed by Francesco Cavalli with the *favola drammatica, L'Egisto* (1642 or 1643) and, in 1650, *Giasone*. In the course of the following years numerous operas and cantatas were supplied by Bertali of Verona, Sances of

Rome, and Ziani of Venice. On the occasion of the marriage of Leopold I with Margareta of Spain, Marc' Antonio Cesti was commanded to produce a grand opera, *Il pomo d'oro*. The new style of writing for string instruments is not yet clearly marked in all these compositions, but we can already find phrases in which the influence of a special kind of writing for the string ensemble can be discerned. This new manner appears principally in the symphonies and ritornelli. The opera *Il principe generoso,* which dates from the year 1665 and has been falsely attributed to Marc' Antonio Cesti (I attribute it, on the evidence of style, to the Pisan organist Remigio Cesti), is an exception. We find there the following note on the orchestra :

Le Zinfonie sono state suonate raddoppiate ad uso de Concerti di Francia, cio à sei Violini, quattro Contralti, quattro Tenori, quattro Bassi di Viola, un Contrabasso. Una Spinettina acuta et uno Spinettone. Una Tiorba, et uno Arciliuto.

As the composer's prefatory note indicates, we have here an example of instrumentation in the French style, in which the two violins and bass are detached from the general string ensemble. This structure is often found in later Viennese scores, but it does not correspond to Marc' Antonio Cesti's style of writing.

At the time of the first operas it was held that the generous use of viole da braccio and viole da gamba gave the music an archaic character. Marc' Antonio Cesti uses two viole da gamba and a graviorgano for the aria of Œnone abandoned by Paris in *Pomo d'oro* and emphasizes its melancholy character by this sombre instrumentation. He also uses soprano, alto, tenor, and bass viole da braccio in the aria sung by Discordia in the first act. Later this ensemble tended more and more to disappear from the scores of secular music, but it was still used in church music, in which style and instrumentation were necessarily more conservative than in opera. A special type of oratorio, also Italian in origin, known as the *sepolcro*—a sort of *azione sacra*—was established at Vienna, where it was performed on the Thursday or Friday

D

in Holy Week. The term *azione sacra* disappeared in 1705 with the death of Leopold I; it was replaced by a more exact name, that of *Oratorio per il Sepolcro*. These works are particularly remarkable for their pathetic style. One of the finest oratorios of this type is Antonio Draghi's *Il terremoto* (1682). It contains an extraordinarily fine ' Suonata a 5 ' for violin and soprano, alto, tenor, and bass viole da braccio with continuo. Draghi's *sepolcro, Il libro con sette sigille scritto dentro e fuori*, written for Good Friday, 1694, has a very original introduction. It has a definite subject, as the preceding stage directions show:

Scopertosi il Ssmo Sepolcro. Si vede l'apparenza d'una parte deserta dell'Isola di Patmo; con S. Giovanni come in spirito e con la Visione da lui descritta nell'Apocalissi. Del libro scritto dentro, e fuori, in mano d'uno assiso in Trono sigillato con sette sigilli: e con l'Agnello che solo potè aprirlo. Precede una Sinfonia grave mista come di suono di Venti, et Tuoni.

This symphony is to be played, as the clefs show, by soprano, alto, tenor, and bass viole da braccio. From this type of oratorio can be traced an uninterrupted line of works expressing the same emotions and similarly scored. At the end stands the prelude to the Sanctus in Beethoven's Mass in D; and the tradition is also to be found in the introductory bars of the ' Adagio ma non troppo, ma divoto ' in the finale of the Choral Symphony—in the dark sonority of the divided violas and the double stops on the 'cellos.

From 1680 the appearance of scores changes under the influence of the differentiation in orchestral sonority produced in Italy. Draghi himself began to pay attention to instrumental writing and gave more exact indications about the parts for particular instruments. From the point of view of style this innovation led to a more frequent and more marked employment of the *stile concertato*. Composers began to demand a better technique from violinists and made them perform passages containing extremely high notes. We now quite often find rapid passages in semiquavers written in increasingly higher registers for the violins. Mention must be made here of Carlo Agostino Badia of Venice, who was appointed director of the orchestra at the Viennese court in 1694. He had a thorough knowledge of the technique of composition and exercised a great influence on the perfecting of orchestral writing. At this period the orchestral introductions and intermezzi increase in length and importance. The part played by wind instruments in the orchestra is reduced, while the violins are set in the foreground. The ritornelli are written either for two violins, viola, and bass, or for two violins in unison, two violas, and bass, or for two violins and bass. In all these cases the *continuo* instruments fill up the inner parts. Badia often uses a solo violin in his arias; examples will be found in his serenade *La pace tra i numi discordi nella rovina di Troia* (1687), *La concordia della Virtù e della Fortuna* (1702), the oratorio *La clemenza di Davide* (1703), *Ercole* (1708), and other works.

In 1700, during Badia's directorship, Marc' Antonio Ziani, nephew of Pietro Andrea Ziani, was appointed assistant director of the Viennese court orchestra. In his compositions he paid particular attention to colour. For example, in the introductory symphony of his *trattenimento musicale, Caio Popilio* (1704), five solo instruments—two violins, two violas, and bass—begin the first bar with a chord of D major. Each note of the next bar is played by two solo instruments; in the third bar all the strings come into action. The result is a crescendo achieved in a purely mechanical way. In an aria ' Sono pocche due pupille per mirar l'idolo mio.' Ziani, wishing to underline the words, uses two viols in imitation. The activity of the two brothers Giovanni Battista and Marc' Antonio Bononcini dates from the same period. Giovanni was engaged as a 'cellist in the court orchestra at Vienna in 1691. It is probably for this reason that one finds in his operas particularly striking parts written for the strings and solo effects for violin, bass viol and 'cello. In his *Ritorno di Giulio Cesare,* for instance, we have airs scored for two bass viols and 'cello and for bass viol, harpsichord, and double-bass solo. In the bass aria ' Occhi belli ' the two solo violins have particularly daring passages which take them up to the highest A. Everywhere the figuration entrusted to the violins is clearly derived from the character and technique of the instrument. Giovanni Bononcini handles the strings with complete freedom; his themes have all the characteristics that we find in instrumental music of the first half of the eighteenth century. His brother Marc' Antonio had less talent; but his style is just as individual and in his use of the different instruments he shows a certain taste and a thorough knowledge of their possibilities. His oratorio *Il trionfo della grazia* contains an aria for Mary Magdalene accompanied by four solo violins, two 'cellos, and a double-bass. In the second part of this oratorio there is a ' sinfonia, vaga e suave, che descrive il moto de i Cieli ' for chalumeaux, transverse flute, bassoon, bass viol, violins, violas, 'cellos, and continuo.

At this period the search for richer instrumentation began to be combined with a desire to achieve a greater precision of outline. Georg Muffat had heard Corelli's *concerti grossi* at Rome in 1682 and tried in his turn to write works of the same kind. In the preface to the printed edition of his twelve *concerti grossi*, which appeared in 1701, he wrote:

Mi venne la prima idea di questa ingegnosa mescolanza a Roma, dove sotta il famosissimo Apolline dell' Italia Signor Bernardo Pasquini mio sempre riveritissimo Signor Maestro, imparava il modo Italiano nell' organo e cembalo, quando con sommo diletto, ed ammiratione io sentii alcune bellissime Suonate del Signor Archangelo Corelli, l'Orfeo dell' Italia per il Violino, prodotte con grandissima pontualità, da copiosissimo numero di suonatori; Ed accorgendomi, che questo stile abondava di gran varietà di cose, mi misi a comporre alcuni di questi Concerti, ch'in casa di detto Signor Archangelo Corelli provai, ali quale mi professo debitore di molte utili osservationi toccante questa nova sorte d'Armonia.

By reason of his activity at Vienna and Salzburg, Muffat was very well known as a composer in Austria and probably had a great influence on contemporary musicians.

The perfecting of string instruments, the standard set by virtuosi of the violin and 'cello, and the elaboration of a new fugal instrumental style changed the character of music.

The clear lines and more extended forms brought about by the introduction of *fugato* banished excessive colour. Rarer instruments began to be used, but their performers were expected to have a greater virtuosity. The Florentine Francesco Bartolomeo Conti, who arrived at Vienna in 1701 as a player on the theorbo at the court, was one of the celebrated virtuosi of the day. His importance as a composer of music-drama has not been sufficiently recognized. His oratorio *David* is a masterpiece which in its day was compared with Handel's works in the same form. It contains an aria sung by David before Saul with a concerted part for theorbo which Conti probably played himself at the performances. Conti, Antonio Caldara, and Fux are the three most prominent composers of the early part of the eighteenth century. Their works prepared for the slow development of a new style, the pure classical style, which has its origins directly in Baroque.

IV

A Festival Opera of the Seventeenth Century

An APPRECIATION OF the festival opera is once
more possible after the creation by Wagner of the music-
drama, in which poetry, music and décor are all forced to
work together to produce a complete work of art. It was
through this that the principle, the ruling one of the preceding period, of the disproportionate predominance of music
over the other two arts, was set aside.

But this Wagnerian conception of the nature and aim
of the music-drama is in keeping with its original historical
status. The first operas were festival performances to celebrate
various occasions at court, and the Venetians were the first
to make out of these a permanent institution for the townspeople. The original courtly character, however, was preserved at the South German courts, where it resulted in an
extremely distinguished, stylized art of opera, whose beauty
can only be understood when the total work of art is taken
into account, though from a point of view other than
Wagner's. For, while in modern music-drama the music plays
the most important part, and the text takes second, the décor
only third place, in the music-drama of the seventeenth
century the most important part was that of the architect.
He had to give reality to the phantasy of the librettist, and
he had to do it in such a way that the weaknesses of the
poet's conception and execution should not be apparent.
The musician had, at many courts, the thankless task of
giving of his best where his efforts were hardly noticed,
though at the Viennese court, where music was appreciated
and many Emperors were themselves composers, the musician
could rely on full attention and recognition.

I should like now, following the inverse of the way in which the historian usually proceeds, to make the character of this dramatic genre appear from a single important example of the festival opera in Vienna. I shall choose for this purpose *Il pomo d'oro* by Marc' Antonio Cesti, which was performed in the year 1666 at the Viennese court on the occasion of the marriage of the Emperor Leopold I to Margareta Theresia of Spain.

History of art, in its reaction against facile biography and an unreasonable cult of the artist and the individual work of art, has gone to the other extreme. It only takes into consideration what in a work of art can be reduced to a general norm, and entirely passes over the personal element. It goes without saying that a true understanding of the individual work of art can only be reached when what is typical in it has been fully investigated. But the personal element, which cannot be fitted into any system, is precisely what gives the work of art its characteristic stamp. In modern works it is only this that we can try to describe. In a work of art of the past the typical element must be distinguished from the individual, as objectively as possible, and both, in the same way, must be utilized by historical interpretation. The *Pomo d'oro* is a sufficiently important work to serve as the subject of an investigation of this kind. It is also one of the few operas belonging to the early period of the music-drama which is available in a modern edition, that of Guido Adler in the *Denkmäler der Tonkunst in Oesterreich* (vols. III, 2, and IV, 2).

The occasion of the composition and performance of the *Pomo d'oro* was the marriage on December 12th, 1666, of the Emperor Leopold I and Princess Margareta of Spain. The exact date of the performance is lacking in all our sources of information about the marriage celebrations and since the festivities, both before and after the wedding, covered a considerable period of time, the most various dates have been proposed. Guido Adler, however, rightly placed the performance during the marriage celebrations proper.

The score of the opera survives only in manuscript, but the Italian libretto appeared in a small octavo edition in 1667 and in small folio in 1668. Both editions are well supplied with engravings of the décors, which are reproduced in the 'Denkmäler' edition.

The full title of the work runs, in the print of 1667, as follows :

Il Pomo d'oro/Festa Teatrale/Rappresentata in Vienna/Per/ L'Augustissime/nozze/delle/Sacre Cesaree e Reali/Maesta/di/ Leopoldo/e/Margherita/Componimento di Francesco Sbarra/Con- siglero di S.M.C./****/in Vienna d'Austria/Apresso Matteo Cosmerovio, Stampatore della Corte/l'Anno 1667.

In the libretto, therefore, we only find the name of the poet. Francesco Sbarra of Lucca is chiefly known as the librettist of Cesti, for whom he wrote several texts before the *Pomo d'oro*. Apart from these there is only the text of a religious drama, an *azione sacra* which the Emperor Leopold I himself set to music.

Besides the poet and the composer, a large share of the work fell to the stage-architect, Ludovico Burnacini, who had to design the décors and machines in accordance with the taste of high Baroque. The twenty-five engravings of the libretto show his fertile invention and his great skill in solving the most difficult problems of staging. He had, however, sums at his disposal which caused amazement even in an age accus- tomed to lavish display. The cost of the décor must have amounted to 100,000 Reichsthaler. Remembering the higher value of money at this time it is not difficult to understand why, even many years later, this opera was still mentioned in all sources as a great event. In order to obtain even more scope for spectacle than the action itself could supply, ballets, whose dances usually had a symbolism linking them to the action, were added to each act. Separate composers were always responsible for these *balletti*. At the time of the *Pomo d'oro,* Heinrich Schmelzer, a Viennese composer of consider- able genius, held this office.

It is easy to understand that in an opera of this period, which must be regarded primarily as a co-operation of the most disparate arts to form a whole complete in itself, music could not play the dominating part. Yet the work of the composer, as the means by which the various elements were combined, was the centre of interest and while poetry and stage architecture did not undergo any real development, the musician always tried to provide something new, and expended, even on the most unrewarding parts of his work, such as the introductory Symphony, the greatest technical skill. But this meticulous care was not, as in Italy, lost in the noisy conversation of the spectators. The presence of a music-loving court and the rules of Spanish ceremonial naturally made any disturbance impossible, so that the overtures and symphonies of the Viennese operas could be of an intimate and subtle character, and need not, as in Italy, be a mere noisy signal for the rise of the curtain.

How seriously Cesti took his task can be seen from the after-word which Sbarra added to the printed edition of his libretto, in which he says: ' No small contribution to the success was made by the music, which was performed by the first virtuosi of this century and composed by *Herrn Ritter* Cesti, Ehrenkapellmeister of his Majesty, who, always admirable in his compositions, was in this unsurpassed.'

The action, with all the complication which the taste of the day required, can be reduced, setting aside the innumerable intrigues, episodes, and minor characters, to a very simple basic plot, which shows that the material was conceived in terms not of drama but of epic. For the conflicts do not advance the action. There are no real climaxes even when the poet intended them, but all the incidents, as in an epic, interrupt the development, and are designed to show the hero in other surroundings or situations. In this case the hero is Paris and the basis of the plot is the story of the apple which Discord threw among the Gods, and which is to be the prize of the most beautiful. The three Goddesses, Juno, Pallas, and Venus, ask Paris to judge between them and, in accordance with the story, the poet lets him award it to Venus, who promises him Queen Helen as a reward. Now the enraged

Goddesses, Juno and Pallas, place difficulties in Paris's way. Venus and friendly Gods help him, and thus a conflict arises between the Gods, which leads to the most varied developments. In order to bring the conflict to an end, Jupiter causes his eagle to carry off the apple, and takes it into his own keeping, to present it to 'the highest Princess the world has ever known,' the Empress. The Prologue had already pointed to this ending, popular in court opera, where the finale usually takes the form of a *licenza,* an epilogue in which the performers pay homage to the persons in whose honour the opera was performed.

In the Prologue, besides the usual figures of Cupid and Hymen, appear the personifications of the provinces and kingdoms of the Austrian Empire, Hungary, Austria, Italy, Sardinia, Spain, America, Bohemia, and the German Empire. In accordance with the personifications, Spain and Sardinia are given to the high sopranos; Italy, Bohemia, Hungary, and America take the middle parts; while Austria and Germany furnish the bass, as the foundation. The Prologue is introduced by a Symphony in three parts which are not yet separate movements but, keeping to the form of the instrumental canzone, lead directly on from each other without a break. Thematically, however, they are completely independent. As far as style is concerned this Symphony has features which prepare the way for the tripartite form of the Italian symphony, although the first part may be thought of as a *grave,* as in the French overture, so that we have a mixed form :   Italian symphony : allegro—grave—allegro.

French overture : grave—allegro—grave.

Mixed form : grave—andante—allegro.

The first part consists of nine bars in 4/4, the second of twenty-six bars in 3/4, the third of twenty-one bars in 4/4, in all fifty-six bars, a piece of music which, for the period, is very extended.

The first part of the Symphony consists of two sections of five bars, the cadence of the second passing into 3/4 time. The first section of the five-part instrumental piece presents

Il Pomo d'Oro, Prologue

in the first bar the thematic material which is carried through four bars in a melodically altered but rhythmically constant form, in which the movement of the bass, downward by steps, and the contrasting upward movement of the middle and higher parts with the motive I, should be noticed.

The second section does not utilize this material. It brings two cadences, one after the other, the first of which strengthens the D major reached at the close of the first part. The second cadence is a repetition of the first *alla quarta alta* and therefore leads back to the tonic.

The second part of the Symphony, in 3/4 time, consists of a courante-like piece in a rhythm which Cesti specially favours and often uses. It begins with imitation but has no further contrapuntal development, for after the exposition

the cadence leads in full harmony to the dominant and the second part repeats the first, but with an interchange of parts and a return to G major.

The third part also begins fugally with a lively motive which is carried through the movement:

Powerful chords break in and are in their turn thrust aside by the motive which works its way up through the parts again. Then, however, they re-establish themselves and lead to a final cadence.

Hermann Kretzschmar was the first to point out that the introductory Symphony looks forward to the nineteenth-century programme overtures, because the first chorus is built up from the same motive as the courante-like part of the Symphony. This opening chorus is in eight parts, that is, it is for two four-part choruses which, in the usual Venetian manner, are used to echo each other. This does not mean that one chorus is silent while the other sings, but that the entries of each come in imitation.

The first chorus consists of Spain (soprano), Italy (alto), Hungary (tenor), Germany (bass); the second of Sardinia (soprano), Bohemia (alto), America (tenor), Austria (bass).

It is a jubilant chorus and opens the work with the promise of festivity:

> *Di feste, di giubili*
> *Sia tutto ripieno*
> *Spariscano i nubili*
> *Dal Regio tuo seno.*
> *E in cielo sereno,*
> *Più chiara, che mai*
> *Diffondi Austriaca Gloria*
> *I dolci rai.*

The décor for the Prologue provides a perfect setting for the words. We see a late Baroque hall of pillars, richly decorated with warlike emblems. Right and left, in niches, stand the equestrian statues of the earlier Austrian rulers. In the middle, on a mound built up of captured weapons, towers the mounted figure of Leopold I. Above him winged *putti* hold a garland. In the air are clouds, which roll away, and in their place is seen the Glory of Austria on a winged horse, accompanied by Cupid with bow and arrow and Hymen with the torch. In the foreground stand the figures, fantastically dressed, which personify the Austrian territories.

In a lyrical recitative which Cesti handles with as much skill as Cavalli could have done, Cupid, Hymen, and Glory praise the happiness of the festival day, until Glory sings an aria full of feeling

which ends in florid coloratura on the word ' ammirando,' indicating universal admiration. Coloraturas are even more frequent in the duet of Boemia and Ongheria which follows:

This duet continues for a while until it is interrupted by a choral movement. Both choruses sing together, and in the pauses of the song trumpet fanfares carry on the melody. The trumpets are, throughout, treated as solo instruments and have a very difficult part to play.

The duet between Cupid and Hymen stands out from the rest of the Prologue:

from which the final ritornello develops.

Now comes a choral movement whose characteristic harmonies, in descending thirds are reminiscent of Brahms:

In these crossing parts Cesti's masterly choral writing, whose excellence was so emphatically pointed out in the preface to the *Pomo d'oro,* can be clearly seen. If we reduce this progression of parts to the simplest outline, the similarity to the first theme of the first movement of the Fourth Symphony of Brahms, which also consists entirely of descending major thirds, emerges clearly:

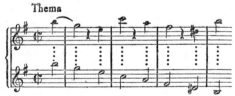

In the further development of this choral movement a new, vigorous motive appears in the vocal parts which lends itself well to contrapuntal treatment and with which Cesti makes skilful combinations:

This motive continues to be prominent and is further expanded in the closing recitative. This ends the Prologue, and the scene changes for the first act.

Act 1.

This act takes the spectator to the kingdom of Pluto. The change of scenery is easily effected by utilizing the architecture of the Prologue. The hall of pillars remains the same. Only the ornaments are changed. Instead of the *putti* we see all kinds of animal figures, instead of the imperial statues, terrifying forms. In the clouds Pegasus is replaced by a dragon breathing fire with Discord, and the prospect between the wide ranks of pillars changes from pleasant meadows to the depths of hell. In the foreground Pluto and Proserpina are seated on richly ornamented thrones. The scene begins, without an independent symphony, with an aria by Proserpina accompanied by two cornetti, three trombones, a bassoon, and organ. Cesti is obviously relying here on the precedent of Monteverdi and Cavalli, who accompanied scenes in the underworld with the sombre sound of trombones, an instrumental effect which, through Mozart's *Don Giovanni*, made its way into romantic opera, where it was even further developed.

Proserpina describes the sad sights which surround her:

The curving line of the melody seeks to express torment, while the long sustained A on the syllable ' sen-' suggests the enduring desolation of the place. The whole aria by its expressiveness, its descriptive power, and the beauty of the combination of instrumental music and voice is one of the most impressive moments in the opera. It provides, too, a good contrast to the festive mood of the Prologue.

The duet which follows, between Pluto and Proserpina, is a lyrical recitative. Pluto asks Proserpina why she complains, and Proserpina bewails the fate which compels her to live far from the light. Pluto tries to calm her, without success, and angry retorts follow, which are pursued in a ritornello. Then Discord appears (Scene 3) and takes counsel with them, how a dispute may be brought about among the Gods. After a duet of Pluto and Proserpina expressing their joy at the plan, the scene ends with a lively ritornello.

The next scene takes place in the palace of Jupiter. The Gods sit round at a magnificent banquet. A stately ritornello introduces this scene, quick passages in semi-quavers indicate the pouring-out of the wine. From the dramatic point of view the scene is important, for the assembly of the Gods is treated not as a chorus but in solos. The short interjections of the individual Gods form a good concerted scene, and make no light demands on the singers.

Apollo drinks to Jupiter in a short arioso. The form is ritornello—arioso part I—interlude—arioso part II—ritornello. Mars sings the second stanza; it has the same form as the first except that the final ritornello is replaced by a short duet between Momo the court fool and Neptune.

Now Neptune comes in with the third stanza, this time without any ritornello at all. Bacchus, Momo and Mercury interrupt, until Momo sings the fourth stanza which is followed by the ritornello. Thus we have a very carefully worked out, self-contained form. Four strophes of the same form are sung to the same melody by different persons, and, to prevent this repetition from becoming monotonous, each stanza is followed by an independent arioso which has no connection with the melody of the stanzas. This is a lyrical treatment, and it is easy to see how, in the place of the *recitativo arioso* of Cavalli which was only broken by arias at the important moments, new set forms are gradually being established whose scope is increasingly widened, leaving only a restricted field to the recitative which must, accordingly, descend to *recitativo secco*. The melody of this stanzaic song is constructed in the French manner, which had already been used by Cavalli in *Ercole* and *Serse*. It flows in an even *parlando,* in quavers, and it is only at the important points that it is given emphasis by ornaments in semi-quavers.

Momo joins in with a rush of words, making the clownish comment that Mars shows himself a doughty warrior at the feast. This passage is, as far as the text is concerned, modelled on the monologue of the Parasite in the *Captivi* of Plautus:

> *Quanta pernis pestis veniet! Quanta labes larido!*
> *Quanta sumini absumedo! Quanta callo calamitas!*
> *Quanta laniis lassitudo! Quanta porcenariis!*

(Act IV, sc. iii)

The comedy of this scene, in the music, lies in the rolling basses, and in the melody rising in fourths.

Now speeches and replies follow quickly on each other, handled with a perfection which is nowhere to be found before this work. This exchange is modelled on the sticho-mythia of the classical drama, where it is intended to represent agitated dialogue. Here, by the distribution of short sentences and remarks among the banqueters, a conversation is realistically imitated. High tension is not, as in the classical drama, the aim, but only the bringing to life of a group of stage figures by a convincing discussion.

How far this distribution of short speeches is carried can be best illustrated by the following example:

Then Discord appears and throws the golden apple among the Gods. Venus, Pallas, and Juno dispute, in an easily flowing trio, to whom it shall belong. It should be noted that Venus's part is always half a bar ahead of the others. Jupiter notices the inscription and reads ' alla più bella.' At this point the instrumental accompaniment is fully set out, though elsewhere it is usually only the figured bass that is given, and, as always at such important moments, the singer is accompanied by strings. This usage lasted until the end of the eighteenth century, and the modern *recitativo accompagnato* is derived from it. The dispute of the three Goddesses over the prize, which follows, does not develop, as might be expected, in stichomythia, but in a well constructed trio, until Jupiter interrupts them, and announces that Paris shall judge who is the most beautiful. The three Goddesses agree, in a short movement, to this decision. Here, it is remarkable that the stately recitative style of the opera deities of Monteverdi is dropped, and a flowing *parlando* introduced, which is more reminiscent of Venetian beauties in a comedy of Goldoni than of Goddesses.

Now the clouds sink down and conceal the assembly of the Gods. Only Momo who stands in the foreground, remains visible, and sings a clownish song on the rôle Paris has to play. This motive, that, of the assembly of the Gods, only the mocker remains, recalls the analogous place in the Prologue of *Faust,* where Mephisto remains behind, and the end of *Rheingold* where Loge mocks the Gods as they enter Valhalla.

The next scene (6) shows Ennone, the beloved of Paris, alone and in a happy mood on Mount Ida.

> *Di Paride mio*
> *Amante et amata!*
> *In terra beata*
> *Ben dirmi poss' io.*

Paris enters and a typical love scene of the Venetian opera follows, beginning with a duet in the arioso style and passing into one in aria form.

They assure each other of their ardent love, then Mercury appears in the air. Ennone has an immediate presentiment of misfortune, and her terror is increased when she hears of the office of judge which has fallen to Paris's lot:

> *Mà quando à gl' occhi tuoi*
> *Pompa lasciva faran*
> *La saggia Diva,*
> *La più grande e possente*
> *La più vaga e più bella.*

The scenes which follow are distinguished by a particularly skilful use of recitative. The complaints of Aurindo, a shepherd who is in love with Ennone, are accompanied throughout by strings and viola da gamba, and dissonances and total pauses are used to characterize the hesitant, mournful mood of the song. It is only necessary to remark that here it is the minor characters who are developed, while the main figures of Paris and Ennone, whose love has a dramatic significance, are treated conventionally, as of secondary impor-

tance. This was perhaps because the composer had to reckon
with a peculiarity of his public, which made them regard the
obligatory love scenes as a necessary evil, and seek relief in the
spectacles and comic scenes. An alteration in this taste was certainly only brought about by the influence of the Neapolitan
opera, in which, in the *opera seria,* the dramatic element was
completely ousted by the lyrical, and could only live on in
the *opera comica.* This, at any rate, is the only possible
explanation of the fact that a scene which is important for
the development of the action is completely overshadowed by
a mere episode. But from the point of view of construction
this scene is of great interest and shows how well Cesti knew
how to provide an instrumental background for the voices.

Scene 11 takes place at the Court of Paris, and is introduced by a solo song by Momo which is intended to give the
singer the opportunity of displaying the mobility of the bass
voice, and is therefore rich in ornaments. As can be seen
from the following examples the ornaments are never mere

embellishments, but intensify the mood by means of 'tone-painting.'

(a)

(b)

(c)

(d)

Here Cesti carries on the excellent tradition of Monteverdi and Cavalli. This is also the case in Scene 13 where Juno appears to Paris. In order to express in the music the solemnity of the occasion, Cesti resorts to a device which is still in use to-day when particularly impressive events are to be depicted in music. This device is archaism. Cesti alters the style of the work in Juno's speech in order, through the associations aroused by the sounds, to produce an impression like that to be found in religious works which use the same method. Harmonized in the simplest way and performed on the graviorgano and theorbo, Juno's speech is extremely impressive.

The aria ' A'i Ricchi quel più ' which closes the scene and
the final ritornello are also of great beauty. If we look closely
at the archaism we shall find that it depends on a free use
of triads on every note of the scale. This is derived from the
best period of *a capella* singing, whereas in the course of
the seventeenth century the predominance of the chord of the
dominant had been everywhere established. In order to allow
of a richer development of the melody the harmony is im-
poverished, and undue importance is given to the chord of
the dominant seventh.

The appearance of Pallas is expressed in an equally significant way. But here the style of the speech is less stately,
and therefore less archaic. It is filled with strength and vigour.
At first the melody unfolds slowly over the pedal of G, then
uses vigorous triads and martial passages, and then passes
to an arioso which also prevails in the march which follows:

in order to pass into a real arietta expressing her feelings of triumph.

But the prospect of military glory has no charms for Paris and Momo strengthens him in this frame of mind in an *aria buffa* describing the hardships of a soldier's life.

Momo

Songs of this type (we remember Figaro's ' Non più andrai farfallone amoroso '), in which comic characters make a general comment on the ideas which have just been discussed in the preceding dialogue, are the forerunners of the typical *aria buffa* of the *opera comica* and the later *Singspiel*. From these they found their way into the operetta. They make it possible for the composer to interrupt the dialogue wherever he likes, even when it is not dramatically necessary, and to give the music free play. From the dramatic point of view musical interpolations of this kind cannot be defended, but they must have had great charms for the public in spite of their irrelevance and their often nonsensical texts, for these songs and *arias buffas* were victorious over the aria and became of great importance in the *Singspiel* and farce.

It is remarkable that Cesti did not use his great talent for melodic invention for the most important appearance, that of Venus. Here he tried to give expression to beauty, in accordance with the Baroque ideal, through rich ornament and florid coloratura. The recitative of Venus, however, falls markedly below that of her predecessors, and wearies with its long description of Helen's beauty, and its endless enumeration of historical names. Here it is clear that the designer, who sets the scene in a luxuriant Garden of Beauty, must have had more than enough to do to hold the spectator's interest. Only near the end are we refreshed by an especially graceful melody with trills.

The answers of Paris, on the other hand, are expressed
with great warmth, and it is clear that he is going to award
Venus the prize.

Act II

The introductory symphony is in two parts, in the manner
of a symphony of Cavalli. The first part consists of fifteen
bars, the second of thirteen. Both are in the same time but
they differ somewhat in rhythm. In the delicacy of the texture the first traces of rococo are already apparent.

Musically, this symphony does not rank very high. The
first scene, too, is rather casually handled by the composer.
It takes place in a seaport. Filaura, Ennone's nurse, and
Aurindo, the loving shepherd, appear and converse in long
monotonous recitatives, but in the last part of the scene
Filaura's aria provides a charming little song in three stanzas.
Harmonically, however, this song is not well constructed. It
lasts for twelve bars and is in F major. Bars one and two
establish the key. In the third bar the dominant, C major, is
reached. Now, instead of returning, Cesti passes in bars four
and five through C major to G minor, in order, in bar seven
to make an abrupt return to F major, a modulation which is
unconvincing, since Cesti is already too far from the main
key to modulate back so quickly. Here we can see the limita-
tions which were imposed on the composer by lack of skill
in modulation.

In the second scene Momo reappears and presents his philo-
sophical ideas in aria form.

Come un   fio - re   è l'A - mo - re   o   ca - pric - cio Gio-ve - ni - le

The third scene contains an impressive monologue by Paris
which is harmonically interesting in its elaborate setting of
sustained and carefully chosen chords. The scene between
Ennone and Paris which follows suffers from its conventional
tone, which is unwelcome after the contrast provided by the
first act. It is only towards the end that Cesti's invention rises

to an expressive duet followed, as ritornello, by an extended instrumental piece whose bass, descending by steps, calls to mind the *lamenti,* the typical complaint scenes, of the earlier masters. The sixth scene provides, after a monologue of Charon, an underworld symphony. Cornetti, bassoon, and trombones give the usual colour, though the music itself is not of a specially sombre character. The conversation of the Furies which follows is also musically undistinguished. The trio tells us nothing of the Furies or of the terrors of the underworld. The ninth scene, composed by the Emperor Leopold himself, provides a welcome change. It was customary at this time for the Emperor to compose single arias which were inserted in the performance of the opera. The difference in style is easy to detect. The style of the Emperor is more vigorous and spontaneous than that of the more lyrically inclined Cesti, and it avoids the long drawn-out phrases favoured by him.

Cesti regains a really moving expression only in Scene 12, in the song of Cecrops's wife Alceste, ' E questa ad ogn' hora.' The melody, with its diminished fourths, is extremely passionate, especially in the second part of the song.

The mixture of the three-beat rhythm with 4/4 also has a characteristic effect, and adds to the charm of the passage. In the answer of Cecrops, the passage 'Che dolenti' is reminiscent of the conventional *lamenti* which originate in the passacaglia.

Che do- len - ti   e pian-gen - ti   Che do- len - ti   E pian-gen - ti

Here it is the piercing seconds which distinguish the passage from conventional usage, and which go to prove that the most ordinary device can, in the hands of a great composer, be given a new turn.

Scene 13 is introduced by a martial symphony. It represents the pool of the Tritons which was the birthplace of Pallas. Athenian maidens, dressed like Amazons, perform a warlike dance. Adrast, Cecrops's general, talks with a soldier and sings a song in praise of Pallas, whose birthday it is.

Then Pallas appears in a chariot of clouds, and two trumpet fanfares, modelled on the toccata of Monteverdi's *Orfeo,* but more primitive, announce her approach. She is in an angry mood: 'Non più pugne giocose.' She has been affronted by Paris, and her anger vents itself in lightning runs.

a mia di - fe - - - - - - - - - - - - -

- sa s' ar - - - - - -

- - - - - mi

The scene ends with a duet by Adrast and the soldier, who swear vengeance on the evil doer. This duet is musically not

Il Pomo d'Oro, Act II Sc. 13 & 14

very inspired, but the unexpected beauty of many passages
lends it charm.

Act IV

The music of Acts III and V of the *Pomo d'oro* is lost, and
as we are here mainly concerned with Cesti's music we will not
discuss the text of these acts but restrict ourselves to Act IV.

This act opens with an impressive symphony in two parts.
The themes of both parts are rhythmically quite distinct, but
they are related melodically. This symphony is, above all, a
good example of the highly developed technique of variation
of the late Venetian composers.

The bass of the first part begins in a slow and heavy
rhythm, which becomes quicker in the sixth bar. This accelera-
tion is really the repetition of the motives of bars two to five.

It is equally easy to detect the original form of the theme
of the second part.

In this second part we find the two outside parts proceeding in consecutive sixths and a sustained inner part, a technique which was widely used.

Scene 1 opens with a touching complaint of Ennone, whose
grief is expressed by the striking use of chromatic alterations.

Frequent pauses suggest the failing breath with which she
utters her words. Diminished fourths and sevenths, in her
cries of grief, show her agitation. The song takes the form
of an arioso over a passacaglia-like bass, which, however,
only keeps its strict form for a short while.

The mood becomes still more intensified when violes da
gamba enter, and, in combination with the graviorgano, provide a sombre colouring. During the instrumental postlude,
Ennone falls asleep. Filaura passes by and, in accordance with
the dramatic principle of the opera, a tragic scene is followed
by a comic.

> *O che pena*
> *O che stento*
> *Senz' haver un respiro*
> *Son quattr' hore che giro,*
> *Come un molin da vento.*

Then she sees the sleeper, and the violins return, bringing
back the mood of the earlier scene. It is worth noting that
the instrumental fabric is built up on a B flat which is held
through six bars. Ennone speaks in her sleep, a motive popular
with the Venetians:

> *Dove, dove è il mio Bene*
> *E qual è la cagion, ch' à me non viene?*

Although the technique is all too obvious to-day, such
scenes must have been very effective in the seventeenth century; or we should not meet with them so often. Here too
we find the characteristic intervals to express grief.

The next scene changes to the temple of Pallas at Athens.
Priests and assistants at the sacrifice form the chorus, led
by Adrast. The introductory symphony has a vigorous march
tune:

A ' Coro dei Ministri ' carries on this mood, which, however, becomes lyrical with the solo of the Leader of the
Chorus. The next chorus is a well constructed *a capella* piece,
which shows Cesti's talents at their best. It begins with chords,
but passes into a contrapuntal style. An expressive ritornello
introduces a solo prayer which is distinguished by the beauty
of its melody.

Pie - ta Di - va pie - ta pie - ta

Pallas appears, angry, in the clouds:
> *Se nel punto d' honore*
> *Atterata son io*
> *Cada pur' anche à terra*
> *Il Tempio mio.*

This, like all Pallas's speeches, is embellished with stormy
coloraturas and the ritornello which follows develops this
angry mood with the vigorous motive

which, with its fugal opening, is well fitted to the situation.
　　Adrast and his attendants take council as to how Pallas
may be appeased. Pallas informs them. She is not enraged
with the Athenians but with Mars, who has been guarding
the apple in his castle since Venus robbed her of it. They must
win it from him with their weapons. Adrast and the chorus,
inspired, raise the war cry:
> *Sù, sù dunque sù all' armi.*

Adrast begins, with a brilliant coloratura,. while the chorus
only furnish the harmonic accompaniment. Then Pallas
sings a defiant song of vengeance which is also rich in
coloratura.

Scene 6 brings back Venus. The stage presents a cosmic scene, the heavens with the Milky Way encircled with blazing fire. Venus is placed in a brilliant star in the centre. There is a short introductory symphony, whose first part is tranquil and solemn, while the second consists of a lively *fugato*.

Venus's aria expresses her feelings of pride in a flowing rhythm. Juno appears and a bitter dispute between the two Goddesses follows.

In this passage the basses, built up in sequences, are striking. Cesti rarely uses this device elsewhere.

The next few scenes contain too little new material to require comment. The first scene worth noting is the twelfth, in honour of Venus and Mars. It begins harmonically and continues, with new material, in imitation. The third part consists of a lively contrapuntal movement which is well handled.

Cupid hastens up and says that it is no time for songs of triumph as Pallas is approaching with the Athenian army.

Venus and Mars sing the ' Presto all' armi' *de rigueur* in the Venetian opera. The Fortress of Mars is attacked by the Athenians. It is a romanesque castle, defended from above. The Athenians try to storm it with ladders, and with the aid of two war elephants. The music of this scene is built up of warlike motives in the style of fanfares. Even the melodies of the singers imitate trumpet calls. Through the decisive intervention of Pallas the victory goes to the Athenians.

With the close of Act IV the music which remains to us ends. We have, as has been said, only the text of Act V. This is greatly to be regretted, for, judging from the libretto, this act must have been, musically, particularly rich. The last part of Act IV can only be appreciated with the help of the stage, and has no absolute musical value, but Act V abounds in opportunities for lyrical treatment which Cesti always makes the most of. The recitative of Ennone in Scene 5 must certainly have been a good piece of work, and it would be interesting to see whether it was an advance on the parallel scene in the *Incoronazione di Poppea* of Monteverdi, the beautiful ' Regina disprezzata.' In the last scene, the inevitable *Licenza* of court performances, the speeches of the Gods provide an opportunity for a choral treatment like that of the Prologue.

For our purpose, the loss of Act V does not matter. There can be no question of a revival of this or of similar works in a complete performance. Our aesthetic approach differs too much from that of the seventeenth century. We cannot forget the lack of dramatic interest, and we feel the linking of the action to a court festivity as harmful to the dramatic unity. Masterpieces like the *Orfeo* or the *Incoronazione di Poppea* of Monteverdi can be performed whole because they are free from such fortuitous connections, and they can still exercise their power on us, just as a play of Shakespeare can. But, if the other works can no longer be performed whole, parts of them can still be given in concert performances with great effect, and can bring back to us a glimpse of that art whose brilliance and riches can only be guessed at to-day.

F

V

The "Balletto a Cavallo"

THOSE WHO ADMIRE the performance of the horses trained with so much skill in the Spanish Riding School in Vienna scarcely imagine that here can be seen the last traces of the ' Equestrian Ballets,' the spectacle which, in the Baroque period, formed the climax of the court festivities. These ballets on horseback, which ultimately derive from the knightly tournaments, reached their highest perfection in Florence and in other towns of Tuscany. On October 27th 1608, for example, on the occasion of the marriage of Cosimo di Medici and Maria Magdelena of Austria a *ballo di persone a cavallo* was performed, in which about forty cavaliers, among them the Princes of Mantua and Bracciano, took part. Another took place on October 16th, 1616, in honour of the arrival of the Prince of Urbino. It was a tournament on horseback, ' The Battle of Beauty.' The music was by Jacopo Peri and Paolo Francesino.

One of the most important performances of this genre, and of importance for the history of the Viennese theatre, was *La Contesa dell' Aria e dell' Acqua,* on the occasion of the marriage of Leopold I and Margareta Theresia of Spain. It was performed on January 24th, 1667, from one o'clock to five, and again on January 31st. The music for the *Balletto a cavallo* proper was by Johann Heinrich Schmelzer; the choruses by Antonio Bertali.

This performance surpassed everything we know of in the history of the modern theatre in the brilliance and pomp of the setting and the costumes, and in the length of the preparations. The allegorical drama was converted to a court ceremonial of the chief nobility of Austria led by the Emperor

The 'Balletto a Cavallo'
La Contesa dell' Aria e dell' Acqua

(*By permission of J. M. Dent & Sons Ltd.*)

himself, who took part in the rehearsals and the performances in spite of the wintry time of year in which, through the delayed arrival of the Spanish Princess, the performance necessarily took place. The rehearsals began as early as the end of August, 1666. Carlo Pasetti, the best stage-architect of the day, was summoned from Ferrara. Grandstands were put up all round the courtyard, itself surrounded by buildings, inside the imperial palace. Opposite the Schweizerhof a little temple of marble, bronze, and lapis-lazuli rose above a triumphal-arch, high above the surrounding buildings. In the course of the performance various machines were used, a ship, a grotto of Vulcan, a formal garden, and a group representing Neptune on the backs of sea-horses.

In view of these erections it is not surprising that 60.000 Reichsthaler was expended on the production of the ballet, setting aside the cost of the costumes of the cavaliers and the trappings of their horses which were provided by the noble performers themselves. From the description of the costumes, which were adorned with precious stones, the head-dresses, topped with heron feathers, the heavily gilded saddles and bridles of the horses, it is easy to estimate the still greater expenditure that these accoutrements of the performers —and the whole nobility of Austria took part—must have called forth. Contemporary documents inform us that this production stripped the Treasury so bare that the means was not left to send even a small troop of cavalry against the Turks, who embarked on a new invasion of Hungary.

The plot of the ballet can be told in a few words. A dispute arises between the elements Air and Water. The Gods take sides, some for Water, some for Air. The argument grows more heated until, amidst battle-cries, war breaks out. The machines are withdrawn and the main part of the action begins, the actual *Balletto a cavallo,* for which the court ballet-composer, Johann Heinrich Schmelzer wrote the music. The simple six-line score gives no hint that, as we learn from the librettist Francesco Sbarra, more than a hundred string players took part, besides trumpets, kettledrums, and woodwind. It must, however, be remembered that the printed opera scores of the seventeenth century only give an indication of the scoring, and that the musician's delight in full, colourful sound was not less than that of the architect in elaborate structure, or that of the painter in rich composition and glowing colour.

For the rehearsal of the processions and the figures of the Equestrian Ballet, Alessandro Carducci, Chamberlain of the Grand Duke of Tuscany, the greatest expert in this field, was sent for. Surrounded by his suite, he also gave the signal for the performance to begin. A fanfare sounded, then a door was thrown open and an elaborate machine, the ship of the Argonauts with sixty people on board, was drawn in. From the top deck Fama, a golden trumpet in her hand, sang the prologue, and announced that the victor in the conflict should have the Golden Fleece, for the greatest bravery. Then the entry of the riders began. Their costumes, heavy with gold and trimmed with lace, and their silver helmets, crowned with heron and ostrich plumes, are described in detail. After a sung dialogue in which the tempers of the opposing parties rise higher and higher Fama sings:

> *See here the Golden Fleece*
> *O you bold knights,*
> *The prize of virtue*
> *And the crown of victory,*
> *Only approach it boldly*
> *Show what honour and high courage*
> *Can achieve.*

Then the ship is drawn off, and the scene cleared for the ensuing performance.

To renewed trumpet fanfares two horsemen begin a single combat in which they discharge their pistols and cross swords. This manœuvre is repeated by others. The engraving published with the description of the festivities shows that the riders followed strictly prearranged lines—that, in fact, an adequate choreography of the whole episode had been provided,

although it did not belong to the ' Equestrian Ballet ' proper.
Gradually all the riders join in this tournament, and the
intensity of the fight increases until suddenly a loud call from
on high brings everything to a halt.

Between parting clouds the Temple of Diana, already
described, becomes visible. Soft music from the chorus,
accompanied by strings, causes the combatants to lower their
weapons and look up and listen to the song of Eternity, which
is heard from the Temple. While the riders, with elaborate
steps, draw back before the grandstands, a chariot of cloud
descends to earth, bearing Eternity and her attendant genii.
Now the clouds vanish altogether and a richly decorated
room is laid open, from which a numerous company emerge,
followed by twelve trumpeters, and finally by the Emperor,
whose costume is described in the greatest detail in the printed
account of the performance. He was dressed as a Roman
Imperator, in a gold embroidered breast-piece, in the centre
of which shone a rose of diamonds and topazes. On his head
was the imperial crown, topped by ostrich and heron plumes.
In his hand he carried the golden sceptre. He rode a black
horse, whose golden saddle and bridle were adorned with
precious stones. He was followed by sixty men of the mounted
bodyguard, then by a chariot drawn by eight white horses
and surrounded by twenty-four lackeys, and lastly by four
saltatori, riders whose horses were broken to the Spanish paces.

This company rode round the scene of the performance
and then took its stand opposite the window from which
the Princess was watching the display, while the chorus,
in the manner of the Byzantine court ceremonial, sang pæans
to the Emperor and his bride.

While the imperial following of six hundred people took
up its position round the scene of the performance, the
Balletto a cavallo, the dance on horseback proper, performed
by the Emperor and twelve horsemen, began with an *Intrada*
in the form of a courante by J. H. Schmelzer, arranged for
twenty-four trumpets, four clarini (high trumpets), two pairs
of kettle drums, and the full body of the strings.

The Emperor opened the ballet, to be joined by his companions. The *curvettes* and *voltes* followed the music appropriately enough.

After these figures the riders took up new positions, and the entry of the four *saltatori,* from four sides, followed to the strains of a gigue in which the strings alternated with the clarini.

These four were then encircled by the rest of the riders and a new, lively dance followed, a follia.

At the end of this the *saltatori* were surrounded by the other riders and had returned to their original positions.

After a short pause an allemande began, played by strings only, in which all the riders took part, in slow and stately figures.

Meanwhile all the young noblemen, the bodyguard, and the lackeys moved towards the temple, to receive the Emperor at the end of the ballet, while the riders formed a cross, at the centre of which was the Emperor. Then the pattern altered. Once more the full orchestra of clarini trumpets, kettledrums and strings began a sarabande.

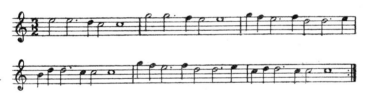

To this all the riders formed a star, with the Emperor as the central point, while the *saltatori* executed the most complicated figures under the window of the imperial bride. To new fanfares the grouping changed for the finale, a formation in ranks, and the marching off of the whole company.

A few points are worth noting concerning the number and type of the dances used in the *Balletto a cavallo*. At this period the first and last pieces are usually marches. They accompany the entry and exit of the performers, and are usually described as *Intrada* and *Retirada* by Schmelzer. If, however, these pieces have the character of any particular dance, they can also be designated by the name of that dance, here a sarabande. Between the entry and the exit most of the ballet composers of the period have from one to three dances, and the order of these is very freely treated. Very rarely the number exceeds this, up to eight.

Here the *Intrada* has the character of a fanfare. The gigue, the second piece, is a gay leaping dance in the Sicilian manner. The follia is a dance of Spanish origin, rarely used by Schmelzer. By the end of the seventeenth century it was familiar everywhere. It is a degree more lively than a gigue. The allemande, too, was rarely used by Schmelzer. Here this dance is distinguished from the rest by the stateliness of the music and the scoring for strings only. The final sarabande is entirely conventional in rhythm, but it is well matched to the opening *Intrada* and consists of fanfares rather than dance music. Compared with other dramatic music of the period these dance pieces show a lighter, less elaborate style. They are occasional music in the best sense of the word, and as such highly valued by the contemporary audience.

If one reads the account of the ' Equestrian Ballet ' published in the *Diarium Europæum* one will at once be aware of the main difference which divides performances of this kind from those of our own day. For here it can be seen that the Baroque theatre possessed in the highest sense the power of binding society together.

In the best period of the classical drama the action on the stage was a festival in honour of the souls of the dead heroes of the nation, at which the priests occupied the first rank of the spectators, and through which stage and auditorium became a unity. In a similar way, in the Baroque period, the theatrical performances of the Court were a ceremonial in which the ruling class acted its own life, its essential character, and its conception of authority and service.

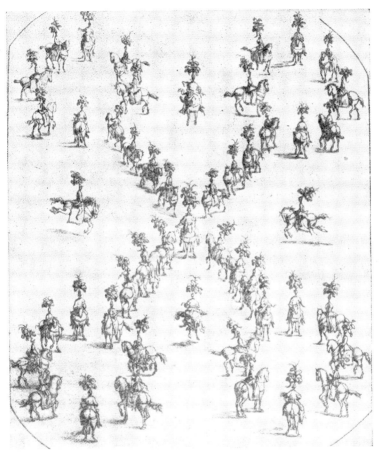

La Contesa dell' Aria e dell' Acqua

These performances were not intended to please an unlimited audience, or to be judged by æsthetic standards. The
standard was provided by those whose desire was to create a
festival for and out of themselves, to give an external form
to the vital core of their existence as it was felt in such exalted
moments of life; through the mingling of the courtly arts of
riding and weapon play with those of the mind, to create a
unity in which they live as well as the play and the players.

In comparison with Greek drama, the Baroque theatre
shows a reduced spiritual significance. It stands in the same
relationship to Greek drama as ceremonial to cult. Yet both
have in common the moment in which what is represented
becomes one with the spectators, the stage with the world.
Ballet, the form in art through which the moment is represented, needs this unity more than opera or spoken drama,
for in it either, as in the present case, the sung word only
comes to the support of the climaxes in the action, or the
singing voice is not used at all.

But within a society which was a structural unity the
knowledge of certain types of material could always be relied
on, so that the author of a music-drama was always in the
closest contact with his audience. It was only when the unity
of the ruling class was broken that the dramatist became a
stranger who was always obliged to provide something new
for a shifting, composite public, and that the idea of the
dramatic underwent that decisive change through which
everything began to assume a problematical aspect.

VI

Three Lectures on Opera

(a) The Problem of Form

O F ALL THE problems of music with which we are faced at the present day, opera presents the greatest difficulties to those who believe in it as a legitimate form and who also believe that it still has a future before it. In a sonata, a symphony or an oratorio the public is concerned only with the creative ability of the composer, and its reaction will be a positive one if the composer succeeds in transmitting his own conception of the work. I am not, of course, speaking of cases where the performance is at fault. I am assuming that the performers will be faithful to the composer's intentions.

It is different with opera. Here, to speak only of the technical problem, it is a question of combining libretto, scenery, production and music to form a work of art in which the individual elements and their combination must be capable of creating a deep impression. It is well known that the best music cannot save an opera if the libretto is nonsensical and leaves the public dissatisfied. In the same way a production which works against text or music can ruin an opera.

Every opera, therefore, is a risk, and every operatic first night a new battle for the composer. This admittedly unnatural situation arose when the operatic composer was forced to turn to a perpetually changing public, and could no longer rely on the sounder judgement of the stable and cultured audience for which operas had formerly been written. This laid a very heavy burden of responsibility on the shoulders of the critics, a responsibility which the best critics would be glad to avoid, regarding their position of intermediary between the work and the public as more important and more fruitful than that in which they are forced to act as judge and deliver a personal verdict.

However, we must take these circumstances as given, and here, as in all other branches of art, adopt the position of the artist, who only recognizes the authority of the creations above which his own work will rise, or to which it is destined to succumb.

This is at the root of the opposition which exists, and which is bound to exist, between those who create and those who pass judgements on works of art. This opposition is stimulating and beneficial as long as the critics take it into account. Criticism is only dangerous if, to borrow a good phrase from Conrad Fiedler's essay on ' The Origin of Artistic Activity,' ' the critic cannot resist the temptation to transform himself into a power to which life and activity must bow.'

As we have said, every operatic first night is a risk. And it is easy to understand that even an acknowledged master such as Verdi, who never faced his public with anything problematical, or likely to excite hostility, should meet every first performance with fear. A detail of the plot which did not please the public, bad singing in some minor rôle, the producer's neglect of some unimportant point, might decide the fate of the work.

Quite apart from these considerations, the question is complicated by the fact that each nation looks for something different in an opera. Without falling into too great generalizations, it is certainly true that the Italian public has a simple conception of opera and, if it is given melodic beauty and fine singing, is prepared to put up with a commonplace libretto, though this must be dramatically effective. The German-speaking public, on the other hand, is ready to accept indifferent singing and the absence of long cantilenas, provided that the orchestra is treated in a stimulating way, the action is interesting, and the scenery novel.

Italian operatic composers have always given expression

to the drama by means of the voices, the German composers by means of the orchestra, and this is still true to-day. Hence the comparatively simple treatment of the orchestra in Italian opera, and the full, rich orchestration of German opera.

If a well-known French composer wishes to have a work performed at the Paris Opera, it is usual for him to submit his libretto for an expert opinion before he starts work on the music. If the libretto is passed the opera is accepted, since it is assumed, and rightly, that an experienced composer will not, with a suitable libretto, write anything unacceptable from the point of view of the stage. The aim of the theatrical experts is, before all else, to avoid the need for the composer to make alterations for theatrical reasons after the work is finished. They also want to prevent a composer expending his energies on a libretto which may have some private charm for him but which has no chance of success with the public.

In Germany, during the period of operatic activity which lasted roughly from 1910 to 1930, a work was usually accepted for an opera house by the highest musical authority, the chief conductor. Acceptance or refusal was based, first of all, on the score. If the orchestration was interesting and there was scope for novel experiments in staging, the opera was accepted for next season's repertory. Whether it would be a lasting gain to the operatic repertory was an entirely secondary consideration. The main point was to have something attractive to offer the public of the often excellent provincial opera houses.

Behind these different methods lie the taste and desires of the public, who in France and Italy demand finish and perfection, in Germany a wrestle with the material, a tendency which has found its highest expression in *Faust*—in the words of the poet, ' Give me the man whose heart is set on the impossible.'

If we take a long period of operatic production in the two chief Latin countries and the same period in Central Europe, we shall find in Italy and France a large number of competent and technically mature works, which, however, never rise above a certain average standard. In the countries of Central Europe, on the other hand, we shall find a mass of works in which worthless and excellent operas stand side by side, or where a libretto beneath contempt has been set to excellent music. An example of this *mésalliance* of text and music is to be found as early as Weber's *Euryanthe,* and it continues from that time until the post-Wagnerian period and the present day.

All the many objections made to bad or tedious operas, all the attacks directed against audacious experiments which have jolted the public out of its sleep, are merely symptoms of one essential fact, the widespread opposition to opera as a form of art by a certain section of the music-loving public, which prefers to listen to symphonic music.

Opera has been called an impossible form and a paradox. It has been said that the events of the last few years are evidence of the failure of the most recent developments, since no single tendency has been followed up, and only a succession of isolated experiments remains.

This seems to me entirely mistaken. The same writers who, some years ago, hailed every new opera as the decisive event of the musical world, regardless of its merit and with no opportunity of considering it coolly and at a distance, now take refuge in complete defeatism, simply because actual events have not conformed to their theories—a fact which tells not against the events but the theories.

Everyone who knows the history of opera and has read the treatises of the contemporaries of Caccini, Peri, and Monteverdi, the first opera composers at the beginning of the seventeenth century, knows that all possible objections to opera were raised then and have never ceased to be raised up to the present day.

How often in the history of opera has it seemed that a dead end has been reached, from which no further development was possible, yet a way has always been found to overcome all difficulties, and to bring the public back under the spell of the world of opera. For opera has won for itself a place in European civilization which it will take more than a few intervals of stagnation to destroy.

We must now look back for a moment, in order to see what were the circumstances which gave opera such a strong position that, in spite of social changes, it is still a living force to-day.

When opera came into being at the beginning of the seventeenth century in Italy it took all existing dramatic forms and welded them together for its own use. Festivals at which music played a large part had been in existence for a long time, but it was not until monody developed that the composer could create a dramatic form in which the singing was continuous.

But opera would never have had such a swift success in Italy nor won such an important place in the world of art if there had existed an Italian school of dramatic poetry comparable to that of Shakespeare and his contemporaries in England. It was only in the absence of this that the Florentine *camerata* could dream of a revival of ancient tragedy, with music and acting, and could see in living poets the legitimate successors of the Greek dramatists, and in Baroque music a continuation of the fabled music of Greece.

We can see how completely a later age had lost any objective criterion in judging its contemporaries, when we consider that the Empress Maria Theresa of Austria, an exceptionally intelligent and cultured woman, declared that the greatest good fortune of her life had been to have at her court a poet like Metastasio, whom his contemporaries rated above Sophocles and Euripides.

Nowadays we know that although Metastasio was a poet who achieved great formal perfection, which was much underrated by the nineteenth century, his work had none of the depth nor the originality of the Greek dramatists to whom the eighteenth century compared him.

Operatic performances in the Italian courts at the beginning of the seventeenth century were events of both artistic and social importance. A modern parallel is the performances of Hofmannsthal's *Jederman* and *Grosses Welttheater* at the Salzburg Festival, where the poet deliberately revived the Baroque festival atmosphere.

The reaction of the public to this renaissance of the Baroque theatre was instinctive. It found in these works a form in which the artist's personality vanished behind that of his creation. Hofmannsthal's *Jederman* became the property of the Austrian peasants. It was acted in the villages without acknowledgement and without a thought of the author, and Hofmannsthal himself considered this to be the greatest success that the work could have had.

The same was true in the earliest period of opera. However much admired the composer might be it was not the impact of his personality but the impression of his work as a whole that was important. It was the *performance* that mattered, the living impression made on the audience by the scenery, the production, the poetry, and the music, as an organic whole. The music had to be beautiful and expressive, but it did not, as yet, occupy a dominating position. Together with the other elements it formed a unity, which was not destroyed until opera became a collection of arias, dramatic material was exhausted, and the composition of operas a matter of routine.

The famous passage from Monteverdi's *Orfeo* where Orpheus learns from the messenger of his wife's death will be enough to show the vigour of these early beginnings. This passage of the score of 1607 seemed to the first modern editor, Robert Eitner, so impossibly bold that he felt obliged to make some private corrections of the original, and it was not until Hugo Leichtentritt, and after him Malipiero, filled out the *basso continuo* that the original version was restored. The dramatic effect is certainly extremely bold in the Monteverdi score. Orpheus entirely deserts the key in which he is singing when he hears of Eurydice's sudden death. The only modern parallel to this ' Oimè che odo ' (Ah me! what do I hear) of Orpheus is to be found in Richard Strauss's *Salome,* where Herod is told of the miracles of Jesus and of his raising of Jairus's daughter from the dead. At the words ' Wie, er erweckt die Toten?' (What, He raises the dead) Herod suddenly leaves the key in which he is singing, as Orpheus had done three hundred years before.

In spite of the success of *Orfeo* and other operas of Monteverdi and his contemporaries, opera would never have been able to take such deep root in the cultural life of Europe, if it had not found, at the very beginning, a secure home in Venice with the opening of the Teatro S. Cassiano in 1637. In its original form of a festival performance, opera was only suited to a court public, and could only be written by court poets and court musicians. If these performances had remained the only ones, the danger of artificiality would have been great. The opening of a regular theatre in Venice, at which each performance involved little expense, placed opera on a new social footing. It was only then that it could exert its unifying influence on society, creating the public of the Venetian opera, which existed as a social unit apart from the actual performances, and survived centuries of change.

It is impossible, and this must be strongly emphasized, to create the same effect by isolated performances, however excellent. A public interested in opera needs a permanent opera house. Continuity is essential, as is also what the Venetians possessed from the beginning—excellence in production. By this I mean not so much an elaborate setting as perfection in singing and orchestral playing, and intelligent and stimulating staging.

Nowadays the technique of lighting and the projection of slides on the stage instead of painted scenery makes excellent staging possible at little cost, and anyone who has had anything to do with the modern theatre knows that the best results are by no means invariably produced by the most expensive means. We may therefore dismiss the idea of a very lavish production, and concentrate on the singing and playing, which cannot be too good.

This was the attitude of the Venetian producers from the

very beginning. Between 1637 and 1700 no less than sixteen opera houses were opened in Venice, and there were always several opera seasons running concurrently. Production and lighting, however, were economical, and only small choruses were used, every effort being concentrated on obtaining excellent singers. The operas produced at this period were, as regards libretto and music, of a high standard.

During the performance the auditorium was in darkness and anyone who wished to follow the text had to bring a candle; servants held lights behind the aristocracy. Boxes could be hired for the season and the patrician families and the embassies had official boxes in one or more of the opera houses where they received visitors and invited friends. The theatre was a social rallying point, the home of witty and gallant conversation, as well as the scene of discussions of the music and libretti of new operas and the merits of singers and ballet. When other towns followed the example of Venice and started regular opera houses, these in their turn became centres of social life. It was, too, a regular part of opera for small groups to collect in the intervals to discuss and criticize the performance, groups which met again after the opera to discuss the events of the evening. This has always been so, and is so to-day wherever opera has a real significance.

I think it is a mistake to underrate the social strength of opera. Wherever operas are performed care must be taken that the performances do not take place in isolation from the life of the town, and that the whole complex, the opera house as an institution, the works performed, and the artists who perform them, should not be regarded as an occasional luxury. Given this, only a few years are needed for opera to become an essential part of a town's, or even of a nation's, artistic life, and this is doubly true to-day when the wireless provides a means of enormously increasing the sphere of influence.

The regular operatic performances of Venice had an influence on the courts and their occasional festival performances. They no longer confined themselves to isolated performances. Every festival was now celebrated by the

G

production of a new opera whose libretto contained some reference to it. These performances, unlike those of Venice, naturally required an increasingly splendid production, greater resources and an increasingly large orchestra.

The opera houses of the musical centres on the Continent were all built with a view to these performances. This brought with it a very real disadvantage. It meant that works of a more intimate kind never really had a chance of being appreciated. Such works required smaller stages, which, for financial reasons had to be connected with the large opera houses. There are now many such theatres on the Continent.

Small theatres of this sort are essential for the production of modern works in which quick-spoken dialogue is combined with lightly scored music. Such works cannot be performed in the large opera house, which can then be devoted exclusively to grand opera and ballet.

Let us now return to Monteverdi and the beginnings of opera, in order to see what characteristics of this early period still survive to-day.

A comparison of Monteverdi's last opera, the *Incoronazione di Poppea* (1642) with the *Orfeo* will show the development undergone by opera in the thirty-five years which lie between the two works. In the *Orfeo* sixteenth-century forms are still used: monologue and dialogue are connected with the dramatic recitative and the orchestra still has the fullness and variety of the sixteenth century. But between this masterpiece and the *Incoronazione di Poppea* lies the great period of the Roman opera and the first works of the Venetian school —setting aside for the moment Monteverdi's own dramatic works—and in the *Incoronazione di Poppea* all connection with the sixteenth century is severed.

This work is a beginning, but at the same time it is so highly individual in style that it can be paralleled by only a few masterpieces. The instrumental parts are reduced to a minimum. The only debt to the Roman opera is the strophic air with variations, which is treated with perfect technical mastery and dominates the dramatic recitative.

The recitative is so complicated that *arioso* passages are already beginning to develop within it, a process which gradually led to increasing importance being attached to the static parts of the opera, and was to end in the substitution of the ' *da capo* aria ' for the strophic air. Octavia's great scene in which she laments her desertion by Nero (Act I, sc. 5) gives a good opportunity of observing the change from recitative to *arioso* forms. We can say without exaggeration that this scene belongs, as indeed does the whole opera, to the most outstanding creations of the seventeenth century. We can still learn from such passages, as did Debussy, who was led to study Monteverdi by the founders of the Schola Cantorum, Vincent d'Indy and Charles Bordes, but we can only learn in the sense that we can take Monteverdi's treatment of a situation as a model, not in the sense that we can copy the stylistic peculiarities of the period. And this touches on a problem which all modern musicians have to face. I want to take a particular instance later on, but first I will state the problem as I see it.

Artistic creation consists in the artist's attempt to give a formal, visible, and audible expression to his thoughts. Artistic talent is something not stable but fluctuating. It is only in moments of creative excitement that the artist can express his consciousness of an interior world of forms, words, and sounds. The value of a work of art depends on the extent to which the artist has succeeded in realizing his vision. I need hardly say that no artist is entirely free and untrammelled in the realization of his ideas. There are periods in which a new technique gives the impression that the artist is completely independent of his predecessors, others in which ties with the past are so strong that the work will seem firmly imbedded in the tradition, and very little different from its neighbours.

The appearance of independence of all previous models is often deceptive, and may be dearly bought at the expense of blemishes which only appear later. On the other hand, a work which at first seemed to be hardly distinguishable from

its contemporaries will often grow in significance and discover
deep reserves of strength within its fabric.

It is impossible for the artist to exist without spiritual fore-
bears; the question is only whether he simply makes use of
his heritage or whether he increases it. This tie with the past
can be a personal one, as the pupil's relation to his teacher,
or that of a young artist to an admired master. In this case
the young man inherits directly what the elder had in his
turn received from his predecessors. Or it can take the form
of a close affinity to a master of the past, in which case the
relation between the two artists will be one of those mysterious
contacts of art which have never been explained. It is possible
to live for years with the works of an old master and to study
them thoroughly without being really aware of their character
as distinct from that of other works, but a moment may suddenly come in which their full significance flashes on one,
pointing the way to new creative ventures.

I must emphasize ' their full spiritual significance.' Wagner's return in *Die Meistersinger* to the part writing of the
Baroque period and of Bach does not prevent every bar
being saturated with his own personality. The contrapuntal
style is deliberately opposed to Walther's free art, and
expresses the wealthy bourgeois life of Nürnberg, but it is
only necessary to think of the prelude to Act III to see what
depths of expression the fugal style and the introduction of
the chorale are capable of.

A very different case is that of Stravinsky's *Oedipus Rex,*
which is considered by many as one of the most important
works of Neo-classicism. Here, for the great tragic moments
of his opera, the composer makes use of elements of the style
of Italian opera at a period when the tragic manner had
been completely overlaid by mannerisms. In *Rossignol,* in
Petroushka, and in *Le Sacre du Printemps,* Stravinsky has
given convincing proof of his amazing ability to handle a
dramatic subject in music. In *Oedipus* he was misled by the
desire to experiment into writing music which does not derive
from the days of the great tragic operatic style, the days of

Monteverdi or Gluck, but from the Neapolitan school whose attitude to tragic opera actually caused the great reaction against opera as a form. These Neapolitan elements he combines with the style of the young Verdi, a style Verdi himself discarded in his later works. An experiment such as this has an undeniable fascination at first sight, but is as undeniably doomed to failure as soon as the technical secrets of its composition are penetrated.

Monteverdi's work was continued by Cavalli, whose fame has been entirely eclipsed by that of his predecessor. But anyone who has had an opportunity of studying Cavalli's works in manuscript must be astounded by his dramatic power.

Cavalli (1602–76) started with the recitative-opera, but even in his early work he tended to develop the lyrical passages more and more into *arioso* forms. The orchestral parts are given wider scope, duets and trios appear, and the chorus once more plays an important part.

Cavalli's contemporaries and successors tended more and more to reduce the dramatic parts of the opera and to increase the static. The rigid forms of the binary and ternary aria dominate the scene. With these composers the days of the music drama are over. Over too are the days of good libretti, when music and text stood side by side, equally excellent. Instead of the dramatic tension being created by the action we find the elaborate form of the aria filled with the various scheduled effects.

Eighteenth-century Italian operas only exist for the arias. Their libretti have entirely lost the freshness and directness of the early operas. The dramatization of myths led to the dramatization of Greek and eventually of Roman stories, and finally of all the important events of ancient history.

The arias provide the excitement and novelty of an opera —the arias and the virtuosity of the singers, who must sing them with perfect expression. But it is hard to-day to understand how for a whole century opera after opera could be written, all dealing with minute variations of the same emotions, all poured into the same aria form. It is impossible for us to put ourselves back into that emotional world and to understand how musical differences, which seem to us negligible, could have had an effect of the greatest intensity.

From the contemporary evidence that we possess we can see what passionate interest was taken in opera of every type, from tragedy to *opera buffa*, from the great festival opera with huge processions and ballet to the little chamber opera with three or four characters.

Side by side with the arias the *recitativi accompagnati* began to play an increasingly important part, and through them the opera tries to find its way back to the dramatic power of the first great period. The first real victory of the *recitativi accompagnati* was marked by the great decline in popularity of the aria opera in England in Handel's time.

If there had been as many music critics in the early years of the eighteenth century as there are to-day, their lamentations over 'the crisis of opera' might have brought about its ruin. As it was, the failure of the aria opera merely served as an incentive to the discovery of new paths, to a new vitality.

It was recognized that the subject matter of the tragic opera was exhausted, and comic subjects were resorted to. But aria opera was admittedly a thing of the past, and composers once again began to pay more attention to the dramatic, less to the static passages of their works. The arias were shortened, the whole scale of the opera was reduced and the orchestra given a more important part to play. We thus arrive at the works which prepared the way for Gluck's reform.

It would be attractive to sketch Gluck's gradual development as a musician who, for a long time, never excelled the average standard of his day, and never at any time possessed a really fertile musical inventiveness; how his artistic conscience, always much stronger than his purely musical conscience, forced him to give his visions that clear form which was destined to exercise a permanent hold on his hearers.

His music was perfectly adapted to the subjects he chose, and it is in this sense that I would call him ' classical,' because he always avoided the episodic, and because his music was in the fullest sense relevant. I can think of no more profound advice to a composer than that which he is reported to have given—that when he starts to compose an opera he should try to forget that he is a musician. Another illuminating fact about Gluck is that he worked for months on the subject he intended to set to music before he wrote down a note, until, in a moment of supreme creative tension, the music of the whole opera appeared to him. After this moment of extreme excitement he was usually ill for a short time, but he was then able to write the whole opera down without further delay, so clearly had he grasped its musical contours.

Gluck, in direct antithesis to those artists for whom composition consists of the perpetual addition of fragments and details, developed the details of his operas out of the whole, which he had already grasped in a kind of vision. This explains the solidity and convincing power of the architecture, the impeccable sense of contrast and the real greatness of his music which made all exaggeration of detail or overloading of the orchestra unnecessary.

As I see it, Gluck, with all his school of followers, has had only one true successor, Beethoven in *Fidelio*. The arias in both Gluck's and Beethoven's work do not hold up the action but are dramatic climaxes, as is the case with the great Venetians and with Purcell.

After Gluck the development of opera can be traced in several different directions. Mozart's genius brought all the glitter of the Neapolitan school to his operatic compositions, and created in *Figaro* the new type of comic opera, in *Die Zauberflöte* the new type of magic opera.

The French Revolution and the Napoleonic Wars destroyed the unity of European society, which had furnished the extraordinarily unified ' opera-going public.' A new society arose in every country, with new ideas. In Austria and the countries with a Latin culture, this process was a gradual one. But in

the small German courts which were to be for a century to
come the centres of a new theatrical life, a new form of opera
grew up, the Romantic opera, with a new subject matter, a
new attitude to problems of form, and a new relationship
between voice and orchestra. It was this new relationship,
starting from Germany, which was to determine the character
of opera during the nineteenth century and the beginning of
the twentieth.

It is unnecessary to explain here how this relationship had
come about. How Jomelli (1714–74) and Traetta (1727–79)
were already using a richer orchestral style than Gluck
(1714–87); how the North Italians, the French, and the South
Germans used a combination of strings and wind instruments, while the Neapolitans and their followers preferred
the simple string orchestra. There is not space to give even a
cursory survey of this development here : I can only touch
on its general aspect, and its relation to modern developments, that is to say, what part, as regards dramatic expression, is assigned to the voice, what to the orchestra.

A detailed study of this subject, with reference to nineteenth-
and twentieth-century scores would, I think, not be a bad
method of introducing young composers to the basic problems
of dramatic composition. I will try to make one example
serve to explain my meaning. During the time that Hugo von
Hofmannsthal was working on the libretto of *Die Aegyptische
Helena* we used often to discuss problems of opera during our
walks at Aussee, and Hofmannsthal was particularly interested in the question of how, as he put it, a librettist could
best give the composer an opportunity for a fine musical
passage. On one of these walks he suddenly asked me, ' Why
is the end of *Rosenkavalier* so effective while the end of *Frau
ohne Schatten* is not?' I thought for a moment, recalling the
two dramatic situations.

In both operas the action is over by the time the final
ensemble begins. In *Rosenkavalier* the trio of the Marschallin,
Octavian, and Sophie comes first, then the duet of Octavian
and Sophie, and the end is formed by the vignette-like mime

of the little Blackamoor. In *Frau ohne Schatten* there is first the quartet of the two couples, the Emperor and Empress and the Dyer and his Wife, and then from above the final chorus of children's voices. Why is this ending not more effective, or at least as effective, as the end of *Rosenkavalier*? As far as the text is concerned it is undoubtedly more effective. What is wrong with the music? Why is the poet's vision not fully realized?

The answer I gave was this. ' Both works use the orchestra symphonically. But in the Finale of *Rosenkavalier* Strauss abandons this symphonic style and gives the voices, in both trio and duet, formal melodies, important, new melodic ideas. An unexpected new invention like this is always effective. We need only think of the final duet in *Aïda*. In *Frau ohne Schatten,* on the other hand, Strauss combines themes from the opera into an elaborate tissue, but the voices have no new material, and, above all, nothing which can only be expressed in terms of a vocal cantilena. This is the root of the failure.'

This is a particular case, but I consider that the treatment of the voice, and the distribution of the dramatic weight between voice and orchestra, is the basic problem of modern opera. I also believe that it is an unconscious revolt against a confused treatment of the voice that accounts for the hostility of the English public to operas written in the last few years. I shall not, I hope, be called a musical reactionary if I say that to-day, as always, everything depends on a clear treatment of the voice as voice, and that only those operas of the Jomellis and Traettas of to-day in which the composer has not trusted his powers of invention but has given the melody to the orchestra and a dramatic recitative, woven into the orchestral web, to the voice, have gone out of date. This is the one fatal mistake, and it is easy to understand the feelings of a generation of English musicians brought up on the madrigalists and Purcell, who prefer not to make the acquaintance of operas which seem to them unworthy of imitation, and directly opposed to their own musical tradition.

But I think that operas of a very different stamp have been

overlooked in England, and that in the last few years Continental opera has developed tendencies which are worthy of notice in this country. A new operatic situation has been created by the conquest of Wagner's influence—but not by the denial of his genius. Wagner's influence on music was like that of Michelangelo on painting, and, in the same way, it has taken fifty years to overcome the pressure of his personality on style and taste, to open up new ways of seeing and hearing, and to make it possible for us to stand free and untrammelled before the problems of opera, enriched, but not bound by the experiences of the intervening years.

(b) Music Drama

IN my first lecture I spoke of the problem of Opera. I started from the principle that opera does not obey the same laws as other musical forms. The fact that it is a combination of text, décor, production, and music, elements which must be welded together so as to make a single, unified impression on the audience, means that opera has laws and aesthetic principles of its own. I suggested that this composite character meant that every opera, from the very beginning, was a problem, and that the seriousness of the problem was in direct proportion to the presence or absence of a regular opera-going public; that if opera is to enjoy real, flourishing health, a regular opera house and a regular public are necessary. I also drew attention to the influence of opera on society in the seventeenth and eighteenth centuries, as it is revealed to us by contemporary documents. I gave then a short sketch of the formal development of music in opera, in order to show how the balance between music and text was gradually destroyed by the growing importance of the former; how a reaction was inevitable, in view of the excessive neglect of the dramatic element, and how the balance was once more restored by the reform of Gluck.

But it was restored only for a short time. In Italy the tradition of the golden age degenerated into an era of imitation.

France, the school of 'grand opera' stressed external display, while Germany, with the romantics, departed from the real essentials of opera in search of new forms and new content. Parallel to this development runs the *Singspiel* tradition, with its tendency to substitute spoken dialogue for *recitativo secco*. This led to two results: either music became less and less important, and comedy with musical interludes developed, or the music became lighter and less serious, and this tendency led to the operetta. Finally, I spoke of the relation between voice and orchestra, which I consider to be one of the most important problems of modern opera.

Let us consider some points which will help us to understand the nature of music drama, as we see it to-day, and its influence on the post-Wagnerian generation and down to the inevitable reaction.

As we look back, it is easy for us to understand Wagner's career as a composer of opera. It resembles that of Gluck, and of both Monteverdi and Cavalli. It is unquestionably the path of a great reformer. To begin with we find works not noticeably different from those of his contemporaries, then new elements appear which lead to the perfecting of contemporary forms, without modification of their framework. Finally comes a period of reflection, followed by a new beginning on a simpler basis. Conventions are set aside, and the new content gradually creates for itself new forms in which every bar is filled with the most profound experience.

We are all agreed that this is the essential question: whether every bar is the result of genuine inspiration. If it is so, any experiment is justified. Whether the experiment can be said to open up new paths is another question. It is often the case but not always.

Monteverdi, in his first opera *Orfeo*, used the forms of the Cinquecento, and in the same way Gluck and Wagner used contemporary forms and idiom in their early work. But in *Poppea* Monteverdi created an opera in which text and music were equally perfect, and Cavalli carried on this tradition. Similarly Gluck in his later operas and Wagner after *Rhein-*

gold succeeded in welding together text, music, and production into a perfect, inseparable whole.

What is it, then, in the music drama as it was created by Wagner that no longer satisfies us to-day? What is it that, in spite of our admiration for Wagner's individual works, makes us reject the idea of music drama as it was formulated in the post-Wagnerian era? I consider the reason to be that Wagner assigned to music tasks which are outside its real province, that he weighed it down with literary associations.

The main cause of this was Wagner's idea of giving to the orchestra the part played in ancient tragedy by the chorus. That Wagner, at the period when he began his innovations and reforms, should want to abandon the chorus, is understandable. He had seen it used in grand opera, where it played a purely decorative part, and he had made frequent use of it himself in his early works. Now, what he wanted to do was to make the individual characters of the drama stand out as sharply as possible from the mass. But instead of entirely abandoning the idea of the chorus and its rôle of interpreter of the characters on the stage, accompanying the hero's words and actions with reflections and explanations, praise or blame, Wagner transferred this function to the orchestra. By means of leitmotives the orchestra was to communicate to the audience ideas and events which could not be immediately understood from the text.

In the first act of *Die Walküre,* when Siegmund sees something, he does not yet know what, glittering in the trunk of the ash-tree, the sword-motive is heard from the orchestra, which explains to the audience, as the chorus would have done, ' What Siegmund sees is a sword. Do you remember? The sword that Wotan brandished in *Rheingold* with the words " Thus greet I the citadel, secure from every foe." You will soon hear the history and meaning of the sword.'

Let us take another example, this time from the second act of *Siegfried.* Mime has induced Siegfried to kill the dragon who possesses the gold from the Rhine. Now he wants to poison Siegfried in order to get the ring, cursed by Alberich.

He tries to persuade Siegfried to drink the poisonous potion which he has prepared and uses deceptive words to achieve his purpose. But Siegfried has drunk the dragon's blood and he understands the song of the birds who warn him, and the thoughts of men cannot remain concealed from him. Wagner lets Mime sing ' Siegfried my son, thou seest thyself, thou must give up thy life to me,' but in the orchestra we hear friendly music. Wagner therefore suggests to his audience ' You like Siegfried who has drunk the dragon's blood, understand the real speech of men, not what their lips say but what they think.' Mime's thoughts take the form of the cruel words we and Siegfried hear, and his attempt to disguise them is of no avail.

This is a really complicated example of orchestral comment. It assumes that the listener does not give his whole attention to the singing and the action on the stage, but divides it between the stage and the orchestra. It assumes, too, that he understands something of the symphonic technique, and that he is in a sense ' musical,' apart from his visits to the opera.

It is not enough for the audience to give their full attention to the melodic invention of a cantilena or to the perfect expression in music of a single emotion, they must also try to notice motives and themes, and be ready for their reappearance in identical or slightly altered form. This attention to detail inevitably prejudices the understanding and appreciation of the musical structure of the whole work.

The composer's most important task is the organization of the structure of the whole work so that each phrase is subject not only to its own laws but to the structural principles of the whole. He must fully grasp the form of the drama as a whole, as a piece of musical architecture, and this he can only do in a moment of the most intense vision, the moment, in fact, of creation, which is the decisive one for all composition. In this moment the course of the dramatic action, as it occurs in time, is projected into space and successive events appear as a simultaneous whole to the composer.

In the early romantic operas it often happened that the
composer allowed himself to be led astray by his interest in
the atmosphere of a single scene into giving it more emphasis
than its position in the whole warranted. Or, even more
often, composers were enticed by the poetic beauty of a
single passage into a mass of elaborate detail and ornament.
Every excuse provided by the action of the text was seized
on to give the orchestra brilliant and characteristic passages.
This gave rise to an accumulation of detailed effects which
told unfavourably on the impression of the whole work.

We may well ask, then, how it is that Wagner's works,
including the *Ring,* are still so effective, and keep their place
in the repertory in spite of the demands they make on the
intelligence and musical culture of the public. The reason is
that Wagner's dramatic genius was stronger than his theories
of construction. But what was possible for him will never be
possible to anyone after him, and all later composers who have
tried to write music dramas have failed.

Wagner's followers, indeed, took over from him just what
was least worthy of imitation, the moments in which the
action of the drama was held up. They assigned a still larger
rôle to the orchestra by inserting musical interludes, the
passionate expression of the recitatives was increased and still
greater importance given to the narrative portions.

We know what extreme importance Wagner gave to the
meeting of Siegmund and Sieglinde in the first act of *Die
Walküre* by means of the orchestral interludes. In this case
the music has to express in sound what is beyond the power
of words to express. This is an unusual case of the highest
dramatic importance, but in *Parsifal* Wagner introduced these
orchestral interludes not only on occasions when words failed
to express the feelings of the characters, but on every occasion
when the action allowed of a short pause between speeches.
It was from such passages as these that Wagner's followers
learnt. They no longer grasped the full sweep of the drama
as a whole, the structure of acts and scenes. They expended
their best energies on isolated phrases and words, they com-

posed only the details of the drama : most important of all, melodic invention became more and more restricted to the orchestra.

The opera, like the lied and the symphony, lost its characteristic, self-conditioned form, which had depended for its realization on the composer's sense of dramatic structure, and assumed a form determined by his capricious interest in certain isolated moments of the action. This emphasis on the composer's personal taste meant also that the characters of the drama were no longer musically independent. They all spoke the same language. This was a weakness to which post-Wagnerian music drama was particularly liable. The Wagner narratives! We know their history. They are descended from the *romanzas* of grand opera. Think for a moment of Meyerbeer's *Robert le Diable*. Wagner makes Senta's ballad the kernel of *Die Fliegende Holländer* and the line goes from here to Tannhäuser's account of his journey to Rome, Lohengrin's story of the Graal, and Isolde's account of her first meeting with the wounded Tristan.

In all these cases the function of the narrative is to increase the tension and prepare for a climax. The case of the *Ring* is different. Here the frequent narratives serve, together with the orchestral leitmotives, to keep the audience informed of circumstances which cannot be understood simply from the action on the stage. Wagner realized that this method of holding up the action could not be dispensed with when he was writing works which were to be performed on four successive days. Otherwise it would be impossible for one of the four parts to be given separately. But to prevent the audience realizing that his method was a technical *pis aller* he took particular trouble over the composition of the narrative passages and used leitmotives as well to give the words additional meaning. Nevertheless, the large number of narratives has always been the great difficulty about the *Ring,* and this is truer than ever to-day.

A point, therefore, which must be conceded as an exceptional case to Wagner himself, was taken up by his followers

and elevated into a rule. The narrative as a means of inform-
ing the audience of events which took place off the stage
became the central part of the opera. I should like to give
an example of this. I shall take it from Hans Pfitzner's first
opera, the music drama *Der Arme Heinrich,* composed in
1895. Here the musical climax of the first act is unquestionably Dietrich's account of his journey over the Alps to Italy
to bring help to his sick lord, the knight Heinrich. Every word
of the account is described in the music. Dietrich's language,
although he is only a squire, reaches a poetic intensity which
would be fitting for a great lord. His account of his journey
over the Alps and his first view of the plains of Italy is so
passionate and full in the music that, as far as the audience
is concerned, it forms the first climax of the opera.

Yet this is a completely false emphasis. It is not of the
least importance for the action that the audience should have
a description of a journey over the Alps. The squire has only
to tell his master as quickly as possible the result—how only
one thing can save him, a girl who is ready to sacrifice herself
for him. The two moments which follow, on the other hand,
really need musical emphasis. First, Heinrich's despair on
hearing that he can never bear arms again and is condemned
to a slow death, and secondly the resolution of his servant's
daughter to sacrifice herself for him. But, instead of being
emphasized, the knight's desperate outburst is much less
elaborately treated than the account of his servant's journey,
while Agnes's resolution to make the sacrifice is not brought
in until the next scene, where its dramatic effect is consider-
ably weakened.

I have given a rather full analysis of this example because
it is not an isolated case, but is typical of a number of music
dramas of this period. Pfitzner's abandonment of the long
narrative in his *Palestrina* is only apparent. In fact what he
did was to raise the narrative to gigantic proportions. The
action of *Palestrina* is contained in the first and third acts.
The story is this: Palestrina has been unable to compose
since the death of his wife. He is now forced to compose a

Mass in order to show the devotional possibilities of his style, and so to prevent the Council of Trent from banning polyphonic music from the worship of the Church. Inspired by angels, he writes the *Missa Papae Marcelli*. This forms Act I. In Act III the Pope pays Palestrina a visit of thanks, and both he and the people of Rome hail him as the saviour of Church music. In between lies Act II, which shows the Council of Trent and the squabbles of the clergy, and ends with a quarrel among the flunkeys which is savagely suppressed. All that this act has to express is the contrast between Palestrina writing his divinely-inspired Mass, immediately acclaimed by Pope and people, and the Council engaged in petty quibbling over words.

There is hardly an act in the whole history of drama which has so little to do with the action as this second act of *Palestrina*. Yet it is always a success with the public because of its richness in theatrical effects. It is only later that one asks why the work as a whole is unsatisfactory, in spite of a number of good moments provided by both text and music. It is only when the work is analysed that the fatal break in the dramatic structure becomes plain.

It is not only when the libretto is at fault that composers of this period made mistakes in dramatic construction. Even in works where the libretto is beyond praise the composer may make mistakes in the disposition of his musical climaxes.

As an example I shall take Richard Strauss's *Elektra*. Hofmannsthal's libretto, originally written as a play, is a single crescendo from beginning to end. The scene with the maidservants prepares the way for the actual drama. Then Electra enters and tries to conjure up the ghost of her murdered father from the ground. She whispers hurriedly with the spirit of the dead man, as she whispers every day while she waits for the hour of revenge. Suddenly her sister Chrysothemis calls her and she wakes as from a dream. And so scene follows scene until Orestes comes and kills Ægisthus and Clytemnestra. Then, in a flash, Electra comprehends the great reality, as though she had done the deed by her

H

brother's hand. For her, divine justice has been restored, her father avenged. But she is overpowered by the event and falls dead after a few steps of her dance of triumph.

This is the story of the original play. Let us turn to the opera. Electra appears after the opening scene of the maid-servants. Her conjuring up of Agamemnon's ghost is slow and solemn, the act of a priestess rather than of a woman on the verge of madness. The music is majestic and heavy. Then she sees the day of vengeance, and herself with her brother and sister dancing round Agamemnon's tomb, but it is no mere vision, for she dances in actual fact to the accompani-ment of the full orchestra at its most brilliant.

This scene is the opera's musical climax. It is impossible for the closing scene to be more effective, it has no new material being only a musical expansion of the earlier scene. Electra's real victory dance falls below her visionary dance.

By this approach Strauss reaches a high tension early in the opera. This tension he manages to maintain in a masterly fashion, without a slip, but the figure of Electra can never be used to create a greater climax. In this respect the opera is a step backward from *Salome,* though *Salome* has not, as far as the music is concerned, the freedom and pregnancy of style that *Elektra* has.

If we attempt to explain Strauss's transgressions of the principles of dramatic construction in this and other cases, and those of other composers famous for their technical mastery, we shall be led to trace the cause of all such over-emphasis to the beginnings of romantic opera.

After *Fidelio,* and towards the end of his life, Beethoven wanted to compose another opera. The Austrian poet, Franz Grillparzer, brought him the text of a fairy opera *Melusine.* The libretto, which has great poetical beauty, pleased Beet-hoven enormously. He was only dissatisfied with the opening, which consisted of a Huntsmen's Chorus. He pointed out to Grillparzer that Weber's *Freischütz,* then at the height of its popularity, also began with a Huntsmen's Chorus, ' and if Weber uses four horns I shall have to have eight.' The opera orchestras of the day could not provide so many horns and the project was abandoned.

The tendency to increase orchestral resources was thus already making itself felt in Beethoven's day, and indeed, influenced Beethoven himself. There was no question of writing a *better* chorus than Weber—an easy task for Beethoven—but one which would be more effective, and sound more interesting.

Berlioz, with all the resources of the Paris Opera to draw on, could realize his ideals. Wagner compelled opera orchestras to increase their numbers. Strauss, finally, in *Salome* and *Elektra,* went far beyond Wagner. The audience was to be stimulated by perpetually changing timbres and tone-colours, with the result, as I have said, that attention was distracted from the voice to the orchestra, from the action on the stage to its symphonic accompaniment.

To return to *Elektra,* it would be possible to maintain that the faults of its construction cannot be so serious since it is still, in spite of everything, one of the most successful of modern operas. But this is not the point. Beethoven's *Fidelio* at first had only moderate success. It won its place in the repertory slowly and with difficulty. We are not speaking of immediate success with the public, but of the highest standards applicable to great works of art; it is only through a thorough understanding of these that we can understand the nature of opera. On the other hand we must not overlook the fact that both public and musicians at the end of the last century, and the beginning of this, demanded this fascination from the orchestra, and did not want to attend to the stage. Nevertheless, there can be no doubt that the future of opera is with those who concentrate, at the climaxes, on the stage.

Even at the height of the music drama's popularity there were composers who had a sense of the right balance between stage and orchestra, but since their contemporaries did not share this sense their works had to undergo modifications which changed their whole character.

Der Barbier von Baghdad by Peter Cornelius, a young friend of Wagner, is an example. This opera was lightly orchestrated by the composer, but was later adapted by Felix Mottl and filled with orchestral effects and additions. It was performed in this version and met with very little success. The public, perhaps unconsciously, felt the incongruity of a light libretto with Lisztian orchestration.

Everything we have said has gone to show the uncertainty of the relationship between orchestra and stage in modern opera. The Baroque opera, on the other hand, had a definite, fixed, musical structure. Even if the static parts became somewhat obtrusive in some periods, the general organization of an opera was, nevertheless, on a firm basis and one which met the requirements of the audience. This solidity disappeared with the beginning of the romantic opera in Germany.

Music drama grew out of quite different aesthetic conditions, and created a new attitude to music, an attitude which is more closely connected than has hitherto been recognized with the whole growth of ideas in the period.

It would be attractive to undertake a detailed study of this question. To show how, during the nineteenth century, a musical idiom developed which was transplanted from the opera to the symphonic poem and then back again to the opera. How, in the main, these musical formulae were given to definite instruments, so that the composer could count on raising definite associations in the mind of his audience by a certain type of phrase given to a certain instrument. This convention made the composer's task much easier. It would be interesting, too, to show how the tendencies of the romantic movement lingered on in music, especially under the influence of the music drama, long after they had been abandoned in poetry and painting. In music there was a second flowering of romanticism. This was the case not only in Germany and France but also in Italy, although Verdi, as has only lately been recognized, never took over the symphonic style of German romantic opera, but remained true to his original principle in his choice of subjects. Certainly, a great genius, as he was, could never have borrowed superficial tricks of style. His was rather an inner struggle with his opposite of the North, and through this struggle he found his deepest self and purified himself of the last remnants of the style of the Paris Opera, so that his last works have all his good points and none of his weaknesses.

I should like to illustrate this point by an example from *Aïda*, Act III. Aïda is trying to persuade Rhadames to fly with her to her home. There in the woods, amongst fragrant flowers, they will be able to live their love-idyll in happiness. Aïda sees the countryside in her mind, the call of home rings in her ears. What an opportunity to play on the audience with magnificent orchestral painting! Think of Pfitzner's *Der Arme Heinrich*. Instead, we find the most extreme economy of means, not a single bar of orchestral interlude, only an exquisitely tender melody, to the words, ' La tra foreste vergini,' accompanied by three flutes with a clarinet as bass. Verdi regarded Aïda's vision only as a preparation for the events which are to follow on the stage, and therefore he scores the passage lightly, relying entirely on the distant sounding flutes and saving the full orchestra for the duet in which Rhadames expresses his readiness to fly with Aïda, and, still more, for the scene with Amonasro and the tragic finale of the act. Details remain details, and that is why the structure of the separate acts and scenes is so effective.

But we must now ask when and how the reaction against music drama began. As we know, it was a reaction against the grand style of Baroque opera which brought comic opera into being; it was a reaction against the aria opera which brought Gluck and the reform, one of whose earliest symptoms was the production of *The Beggar's Opera* in England. It might therefore have been expected that an intensive cultivation of comic opera should succeed the music drama. But this time the reaction took a more complicated form. It might have been expected to start from England, which was fortunate enough to possess in Gilbert and Sullivan a combination of musician and librettist which made comic opera possible. But Gilbert's libretti were too witty for continental taste, and Sullivan's music too light for an audience brought up to admire romantic opera. In Germany, on the other hand, *Die Meistersinger* had such an effect on German composers that it was impossible for them to produce a really natural and light-hearted opera of their own in Wagner's life-time, or immediately after his death.

The Czech school, whose chief representatives were Smetana and Dvořák, produced a series of popular works. *The Bartered Bride* is a masterpiece of its kind, and Dvořák's *Kate and the Devil* is a successful popular piece. But there is one masterpiece of comic opera in the true sense of the term, which belongs to this period: Verdi's *Falstaff*. It appeared twelve years after Wagner's death and is untouched by the slightest trace of Wagnerian influence. It was the work of a composer whose success was second only to Wagner's but it had itself little success.

It was not until later that a comic opera succeeded in winning a permanent place in the repertory. This was *Rosen-kavalier*.

From the correspondence between Strauss and Hofmanns-thal it is clear that after *Elektra* Hofmannsthal made every effort to induce Strauss to abandon the path he had followed in this opera. He wanted to make Strauss take up the thread where Mozart had left it. Only a poet whose whole character and attitude to art were in direct opposition to Wagner could hope to open up a new path for Strauss. And if Strauss had not had a deep leaning towards Mozart, Hofmannsthal's efforts would have been fruitless. But Strauss's affinity had been evident in his performances of Mozart, and now his talent, given full play by the special nature of the text of *Rosenkavalier,* was able to unfold naturally and to produce the most successful comic opera of the modern repertory. But neither this type of comic opera, nor the fairy opera, nor the realistic opera such as Charpentier's *Louise,* nor even Debussy's *Pelléas et Mélisande,* constitute a reaction against music drama comparable to the reactions of earlier periods.

The reason is that the music drama as it was propagated by Wagner was a revolutionary form with which his age had come to terms. The real reaction against music drama could not begin until new dramatic forms had come into being and had exerted an influence on the opera-going public. These forms were the chamber opera, in which the main emphasis shifted naturally from the orchestra to the stage, and the ballet.

It was during the transitional period that *Ariadne auf Naxos* appeared, the joint work of Strauss and Hofmannsthal. This was the first opera in which a really notable attempt was made to alter the prevailing relationship between voice and orchestra. Whereas the ultimate failure of many operas of the period may be put down to the libretto, in the case of *Ariadne* success was undoubtedly due to the influence of the libretto on the musical form and the production. It was thanks to the libretto that the first chamber opera appeared, as it were by chance, and to no fixed programme.

Originally, *Ariadne auf Naxos* was conceived as an interlude in *Le Bourgeois Gentilhomme,* a ' thirty minute opera,' as Hofmannsthal puts it in a letter. But as composer and poet worked on it the opera assumed larger proportions—too large for the original purpose. It is a parallel case to that of the *Serva Padrona* of Pergolesi, an intermezzo which, separated from the forgotten *opera seria* to which it once belonged, became world famous.

The whole work, however had to be rewritten for its new function. The running together of the two plots must be somehow accounted for, and this need produced the charming prelude, written with a definite end in view. Hofmannsthal felt that Zerbinetta, with her big coloratura aria, was not in strong enough contrast to Ariadne. He therefore wrote the scene in which she turns the young composer's head and makes him obey the patron's command to give *opera seria* and comedy together. Through this preparatory scene Zerbinetta becomes a real dramatic figure. As the work stands, the contrast between Ariadne and Zerbinetta is parallel to the contrast between Mignon and Philine in Goethe's *Wilhelm Meister*.

The fact that *Ariadne* was originally intended for production with Molière's play in a theatre with only small accommodation for orchestra, led Strauss to use a small orchestra for the first time. The second version appeared in 1916, and with it the first important chamber opera.

We must now turn our attention to the ballet. To understand its position, or rather that of dancing on the stage, as part of the reaction against music drama, we must leave opera for a moment and consider the position of music in general at the end of the romantic period.

There were two opposing schools. One concerned itself more and more with psychological problems, the other frankly catered for the popular taste. The former tended to become more and more exquisite and spiritualized. The latter had no aim but to be generally acceptable. This was a new cleavage in the world of music, and the longer it lasted, as an opposition of serious and light music, the more dangerous it became.

Progressive musicians were forced to take deliberate measures to counteract the reduction by the ' light ' composers of all emotion to the level of the banal. They did this by developing an increasingly reticent and difficult musical idiom and by surrounding themselves with all the mysteries of their craft. Nineteenth-century music became increasingly intellectualized. Between the speech of the composer and the audience a third element was interposed. This was the literary ' key ' to the musical composition. The most flagrant examples of it was the printed programme or programme notes provided to interpret orchestral works.

Dancing, on the other hand, is an art of the moment. The dancer can only represent the events and emotions of the dramatic action as it takes place on the stage. Therefore music for the ballet must concern itself entirely with the events of the particular moment and situation. Formally and rhythmically it must be precise, unreflective, and without thematic combinations to which nothing in the choreography corresponds. Ballet music can have none of the characteristics of programme music, none of the epic-narrative passages of romantic opera, nor can the personality of the composer play in it the large part which it played in the ' absolute,' as well as the dramatic, music of the nineteenth century.

The Russian Ballet had all these characteristics. An unusual school of dancing, new type of scenery, and new production were combined with a vigorous music whose rhythmic energy was completely new. The visits of the Russian Ballet to the capitals of Western Europe and to America—I am speaking of the years just before the first World War—were a revelation to all those who were looking for a way of escape from post-Wagnerian music drama. Here, it was clear, were new possibilities of dramatic characterization, capable of imparting a new life to the operatic stage.

The stage and the action on it were once more restored to a position of importance. Once more an intimate connection was established between the dancer's movements and the music. In future the usual clumsy and meaningless gestures of singers on the stage were intolerable. The chorus too, with its conventional gestures without connection with the drama, could no longer be endured. They were required to act as a stylized crowd, and expected to take part in the action, even when they had nothing to sing. The action on the stage had to give the impression of a finished composition in which nothing was left to individual caprice. The human being, not the details of a room or landscape was once more the centre of the stage.

This renaissance of the stage was not confined to modern works. Its principles were applied to earlier ones. I once compared the old and the modern sketches for Wagner's operas. In the old ones the singers are lost in their surroundings. Siegfried is obscured by the forest. Klingsor vanishes behind the realistic apparatus of his magician's den. In the modern sketches detail plays only a small part. The scenery is only intended to provide a background for the action and

the characters. This, and the recognition of the importance of
the actors' movements has led to a new practice. The scenery
is no longer entrusted to a painter, who aims at the greatest
possible pictorial charm and historical accuracy, but who
knows nothing either of music or stage managing. Instead the
practice of Baroque opera has been adopted and the scenery
is given to a stage architect, who works with the producer.
His first task is to make the best possible disposition of the
available space. According to the present practice the producer first makes a sketch for each scene, taking careful
account of the entrances of each character, and then the
architect makes the coloured models and sketches the dresses,
which must fit the colours of the scenery.

The generation which fought for Wagner and the music
drama rated the ballet low, and rightly. The ballet they knew
represented the decadence of an art which had flourished
until the end of the eighteenth century. The Russian Ballet
combined an unexpected renaissance of the old ballet with
some new elements. This was the secret of its greatness. I
shall have to speak later of the extraordinary interest in ballet
which the Russian Ballet excited in Germany. Unfortunately
one of the greatest ballerinas brought about a new divorce of
dancing and music by starting a school of dancing unaccom-
panied, or accompanied only by percussion instruments. The
development of ballet was side-tracked by this separation from
music, and the new path was soon seen to be a blind alley.
But the split with the operatic stage had taken place. If this
new movement had remained in touch with music, as the
Russian Ballet did, it might have had great results. As it is,
there have only been isolated attempts, attempts in which I
myself have been concerned, to create new works for the
operatic stage with the help of ballet. Dancers, however, are
generally even more fanatical than prima donnas on the subject of the complete independence of their private interpretation of their rôle from the work as a whole. They are unwilling
to submit to the ordinary opera house regime and can come
to no understanding with the existing corps de ballet. For

these reasons many of the smaller opera houses have ceased to maintain a corps de ballet.

Nevertheless, as I have said, it was impossible to forget the effect of ballet on the décor of opera, and there is no doubt that it recalled a whole generation to their senses and pointed the way to new paths for opera.

(c) The Latest Development of Opera

HOWEVER obvious, and even platitudinous, it may sound baldly stated, I must stress once more the fact that opera cannot be judged by the music alone. For this reason it is concerned not with the music-loving public in general, but with a specific opera-going public, whose interest is not in the music or the plot of a work, but in the opera itself, and its peculiar atmosphere, an atmosphere hard to describe, that of a world within our ordinary world of everyday happenings. Not that all connection with reality is severed. Indeed, the greatest operas represent a world on the border-line between imagination and reality.

Opera has no uniform development. The relation of its component parts to each other is perpetually shifting. A period in which the dramatic element is exaggerated is followed by one in which text and music have equal rights. An era in which the stage is neglected is followed by one in which special attention is paid to it.

The creative faculty is a mystery. We know that the production of a work of art depends not only on its possession by the artist, but also on the presence of circumstances favourable to its development. The wider are the horizons of a young artist the easier his development will be. The hindrance of unfavourable circumstances, exterior or interior, will prevent the creation of anything original or significant, however rich the artist's potentialities may be.

The absence in England, for example, of a regular opera is certainly a case of unfavourable exterior circumstances which prevented the full development of much potential dramatic talent. In eighteenth-century Italy, on the other hand, the existence of numerous opera houses made it possible for even minor dramatic talent to develop fully. For an example of interior hindrance we have only to think of the effect of the music drama on the music of the late nineteenth century. All over the Continent the horizon of the musician was narrowed, and composers were led to choose dramatic sub-jects which were unsuited to their individual gifts and which prevented the full development of their talent. What was wanted was musical teaching equivalent to the work of young painters in museums, who study examples of the great masters of every age and school, so that musicians could have the opportunity of direct stimulus, and, what is more important, the stimulus of contact with talents congenial to their own.

Debussy provides an example of the effect of this kind of stimulus. He was in no sense at home in the post-Wagnerian era and it was under the most varying influences that he finally discovered his own individual language and with it the whole wealth and charm of his musical nature. As I see it his fundamental characteristic was a highly developed sense of logic and proportion both in form and expression. His early works only hint at his real talents. In them his musical idiom is an extremely restricted form of the language of Chopin and Schumann. It was his meeting with Mallarmé that first showed him the way to the real depths of his own artistic nature and gave him a goal to aim at.

His attitude to music was that of the Mallarmé group to poetry and painting. In the Schola Cantorum he learnt to know Gregorian music just on the eve of the Solesmes revival. Here too, he came into contact with Monteverdi's dramatic style. Saint-Saëns introduced him to Mussorgsky's *Boris Godunov,* and this had a decisive influence on his dramatic technique. At the Paris World Exhibition of 1900 he heard the music of the Far East, which gave his piano works their exotic flavour and suggested to him the rich soft harmonies and the use of the whole tone scale characteristic of his middle period. Finally, his rhythms were influenced by Spanish and

Russian music. In his last period he returned to the great musical ancestors of his own country, Rameau and Couperin, and his sonatas show a new simplicity of style which only mature genius can achieve.

These were influences of the most diverse kinds, and ones which might have been dangerous to a lesser talent or, even more, to a less emphatic personality. But for Debussy each one contributed to the unfolding of his potential genius and served to nourish his artistic personality, which without these stimuli would have remained one-sided and limited.

Isolation seems to me very dangerous, particularly for a young musician, whose whole development may be prejudiced by it. The immense number of unperformed operas at the end of the last and the beginning of the present century shows that talent and the mastery of academic technique by themselves lead nowhere. Every artist must develop himself in the highest sense. He must first learn from his great predecessors and then try to find himself, his own personal message and idiom. If he does not do so, he will share the fate of so many gifted musicians, and especially opera composers, who have been ruined by undertakings for which they were not suited.

Nevertheless, a clear distinction must be made between an artist who studies the old masters, and through them finds his own style, and one who appropriates technical devices peculiar to another, a proceeding which has nothing to do with an artist's inner development. Such appropriation is, unfortunately, exceedingly common.

I may perhaps mention here an episode which occurred to me personally in 1923 in Paris. It was after the first performance of Stravinsky's *Mavra*, a small opera of the Neapolitan type, a complete change from his earlier works, and harmonically of a deliberately exaggerated simplicity. Admirers of his earlier works were, therefore, slightly puzzled. I was standing in front of the theatre after the performance with a small group of musicians, when one of them, who up to that moment had been silent and apparently lost in thought, suddenly spoke. Half to himself, half to the others, as one liberated from a great burden, he said, ' So now we can write common chords again.'

Such a remark, however absurd it may seem at first sight, is characteristic of our day and of the attitude of young second-rate composers to their heroes, especially of a certain group of Stravinsky's admirers who were ready to follow blindly any of his stylistic *voltefaces* without pausing to consider what inner necessity had caused them. Their attitude to these changes was like their attitude to changing fashions— ' Common chords are worn again now.'

Both the heroes and their devotees assume a great responsibility in representing incidental technical novelties as the essential part of a work of art. It would be unpleasant to think that their reason for doing so was simply that in their own works externals are the essential part.

This mentality is undoubtedly a symptom of great instability in artistic taste, and it is this instability on the part of composers, critics, and public alike which accounts for the many abortive experiments made in the musical world in the last few years. In an era in which all fundamental principles are called in question, art itself, and especially such a problematic art-form as opera, could hardly expect to escape being drawn into the whirlpool. We, as artists and friends of the arts have to find our own feet in this insecurity, and make sure that each one of us fulfils the part for which he is fitted, to which he is impelled by the inner necessity of his nature. That is all we can do to help the world of music to regain security. We shall only find a firm foothold in the shifting sands, an abiding place in the midst of change, when we can see the work of art as the essential expression of the artist.

But we must leave these general considerations and turn to the subject of this lecture. We must start from this very insecurity, which is the most striking characteristic of art and the approach to art at the beginning of the present century. We have seen that in opera this insecurity made itself felt in the growing cleavage between composer and public, a cleavage which had begun during the romantic period but which now assumed even larger proportions. Musical form, as we have seen, was destroyed by over-elaboration of detail; the desire for violent contrasts led composers to shift the emphasis from the voice to the orchestra, from the action to its symphonic accompaniment. In each separate case the question always recurs of what dramatic action can be set to music, of what a libretto should be. The relation between composer and librettist becomes more and more difficult. The Italians are still really the best off. They still have libretti in which the link with the old tradition has never been broken. German composers are the worst off, overshadowed by the figure of Wagner. It was a revolt against the banality of opera libretti which led Richard Strauss to compose the whole of a drama written for the ordinary stage. This was a method which might succeed in individual cases but not one which could ever lead to a new operatic idiom.

Goethe once said that ' a work which is to be set to music must be loosely knit,' a principle which Hofmannsthal adopted in his collaboration with Strauss. This collaboration was a godsend to Strauss, but most of the composers of the period were perpetually faced with the problem of finding a suitable libretto. They were seldom fortunate enough to do so. This perpetually recurring difficulty led to the desire for some definite standard to apply, and it was found in a preoccupation with the past.

A cry of ' Back to Mozart ' arose about 1910, among composers who recognized the failure of contemporary opera, but had no power to find a cure for it. A mere return to the past, however, can never create anything new.

Far more important were the efforts of the opera houses to enlarge and consolidate their repertories by model performances of works of the past. The repertory of the Vienna Opera was increased by Gustav Mahler. His performances of Gluck and Mozart led to their adoption into the regular repertory. Lully and Rameau were performed by the Paris Opera. In England, Rutland Boughton performed Purcell's *Dido and*

Aeneas with the Glastonbury players, and Professor Dent produced the *Fairy Queen* in Cambridge in 1911. And there were many other performances here which gave new life to a great past.

Nevertheless, this retrospective movement, however important it may have been as a stimulus, was not itself motivated by any one central idea. A stronger impulse was needed to bring about a real regeneration, and this impulse came from the dance.

In 1910 the Russian Ballet made a tour of Central and Western Europe, with works of modern Russian composers, among them Rimsky-Korsakov and Stravinsky. These performances opened a new horizon. Once again the action on the stage was the important thing. Here was a simple plot, innocent of details, and a rhythmical music in a precise and rigid form, the very antithesis of the Wagnerian 'endless melody' of the music drama.

Between 1910 and 1925 the influence of the Russian Ballet led to a great revival of ballet in general, and the presence of such excellent dancers naturally suggested to French and English composers the idea of trying their skill in ballet music. While this was happening in the West of Europe another movement was taking place in the many theatres of Germany. It was during the period immediately after the first World War, and I must discuss it in some detail, as it is far less well known than anything connected with the Russian Ballet.

Before the war of 1914 to 1918 the dramatic performances of Jacques-Dalcroze and his pupils in Hellerau had aroused great interest in ballet throughout Germany. Immediately after the war Rudolf von Laban founded a new school of dancing based on a return to the old French style, and, particularly, to Noverre. At the same time a group of young producers experimented with a new dramatic style, and chose for their purpose operas of Handel, whose style seemed to them best suited to the ideal of drama they had in mind.

Here in England, Handel means the coming of the Italian opera, the end of a great tradition. Every discussion of opera in England must centre round the appearance of Handel. It was strange, therefore, that it should be a revival of Handel's operas which influenced the operatic stage in Germany and prepared the ground for a new flowering of opera. Certainly Handel and the English public would have been astonished if they had seen his operas as they were produced in Germany, just as the Greeks might have found it difficult to recognize in an early seventeenth-century opera the revival of ancient tragedy.

The operas produced were *Giulio Cesare, Rodelinda,* and *Ottone.* In the new arrangements everything which held up the action was omitted, the arias were shortened, the recitative reduced to the minimum and the text extremely well translated.

The beginning of the ' Handel Movement,' as it came to be called, can be traced to the student performances of Göttingen. The production was based on the principle of giving the singer of an aria *one* single, statuesque gesture which corresponded to the emotion expressed in the music, or, in the case of movements, the dancer's principle of taking his cue from the music was adopted. The contrast between the static and the dynamic parts of the opera was preserved. What was seen on the stage always tallied with the music heard.

The effect of the Handel Festivals was great. Between 1920 and 1926 the principle of operatic production changed in Germany. Young producers, often fresh from the university, tried to produce operas of Handel, and also of Monteverdi and Gluck, on the Göttingen model. Some of them had also learnt from Mahler's performance in Vienna of Gluck's *Iphigenia in Aulis* and Bruno Walter's performance of the same work later on in Munich, and his Salzburg performances of *Don Giovanni, Orfeo* and *Oberon,* and, in spite of the incomparably smaller resources at their disposal, their enthusiasm often overcame inadequacies in the performance.

The revival of Handel's operas, however, was not only a retrospective movement, as it might have seemed at first, but gave a new impulse to some operatic composers. It is

I

significant that from the moment when new operas inspired by this spirit began to be written, Handelian operas gradually disappeared from the stage. They had fulfilled their function.

But opera houses needed works which would attract the public and renew interest in their old repertories, and in consequence the lesser known operas of Verdi, in new adaptations, began to be popular. The Handel performances unquestionably prepared the way for the Verdi renaissance. In both cases the problem was to find a new way of presenting works in which the vocal part is the most important, and the orchestra does not follow the exact outline of the action with the Wagnerian ' endless melody ' and psychological comment, but accompanies the voices.

The difference between the Handel and the Verdi renaissance can be summed up in the following way : the Handel renaissance sprang from a desire for the old synthesis in opera, as it had existed before the breach between composer and composition, which began in the romantic period, had come about. It sprang from a conviction of the high mission of the theatre as something which, whether in comedy or tragedy, must improve the audience, in the same way as the ancient theatre of the Greeks. For the Handel renaissance the theatre was a solemnity, a festival. The chief aim of the Verdi renaissance, on the other hand, was to bring back the days of grand opera with all its pomp, its star-singers, and its exciting dramas. It appealed to a public which looked for distraction and amusement in the theatre and expected beautiful melodies in an opera. Both movements justified themselves by leading to a number of interesting new performances, for both provided a frame within which new operas of one type or the other could develop.

I cannot deal in detail with the creations of the last twenty years. I have myself been actively concerned in operatic production and my personal likes and dislikes would inevitably appear. I must content myself, therefore, with giving you a few ideas on the way in which opera seems to me to have developed.

It will be best to deal first with those composers who had already written dramatic works before the period 1920 to 1930, composers that is to say, whose real worth was not appreciated until some time after their compositions first appeared. The earliest of these works is Mussorgsky's *Boris.* Its triumphal progress through the opera houses of the world only began a short time ago. Only some fifteen years ago was its real genius recognized. Then there is, for example, Janáček's *Jenufa,* a work which, in spite of its popular nature, still shows great artistic abilities and has never been excelled by Janáček in his later operas, interesting as they are. Schönberg's two small one-act operas must also be mentioned, *Erwartung* (1909) and the *Glückliche Hand,* finished in 1913. Both are extremely interesting attempts to compress the action in opera as much as possible. Both seemed impossible to produce before 1920 but in the new era they justified their existence by a few performances here and there. Stylistically, they are interesting as preparing the way for Berg's *Wozzeck.*

Bartók's *Duke Bluebeard's Castle* has certain characteristics in common with Janáček's *Jenufa,* especially the use made of folk tunes. But the two works are fundamentally different in character. Both, however try to imitate in the vocal line colloquial speech, Czech and Hungarian.

Busoni's *Arlequino* and *Turandot* and Stravinsky's *Rossignol* are examples of the return to classical forms, but in each case the libretto lacked sufficient dramatic power to grip the audience, and the same is true of Malipiero's *Sette Canzoni.* In *Ariadne,* on the other hand, Strauss was fortunate enough to have a text full of variety, and this explains the popularity, second only to that of *Rosenkavalier,* which it gained in spite of its high claims as a work of art. When it first appeared in 1912 it certainly appealed to a very different public to that of 1920 and after, the period of its great success.

But although, if we judge by its orchestra, *Ariadne* is a chamber opera, it is really a work which stands alone, and it was not possible for it to influence the new movement very profoundly or to hasten the general appreciation of chamber opera and chamber ballet.

The most conclusive argument for the reduction of the orchestra was, indeed, the enforced economy of the years immediately after the first World War, which encouraged the production of works which did not demand large orchestral or theatrical resources.

Nor was a work like *Les Noces* really influential. True, its orchestral demands—four pianos and percussion—were such that it could always be performed without great expense in this quarter. But on the stage it required the full apparatus of the Russian Ballet. All that can be said is that it was certainly easy for the Russian Ballet to produce, since it needed no orchestra, but it was not within the reach of other companies.

More important were Stravinsky's *Le Renard* and *Histoire d'un Soldat*. They were designed for a small space and could be performed in any small room with a stage. They only required a few actors. This was particularly true of *Histoire d'un Soldat,* which opened up a new path and seemed to promise much for the future, and which did actually prove a work accessible to the public.

In 1920 a new name appeared in German music : Hindemith. His first dramatic success was at Stuttgart in 1921 with his three one-act operas *Sancta Susanna, Mörder, Hoffnung der Frauen,* and *Nusch-Nuschi.* The texts are unusual, and the music, vigorous and rhythmically bold, is closely related to Hindemith's own chamber music.

Almost simultaneously an opera of mine appeared in Frankfurt and Hanover. This was *Prinzessin Girnara,* with a libretto by Jacob Wassermann, who tried in this work to represent the gradual change in the chief characters under the influence of the circumstances in which they find themselves. The interest of the work is not in men's actions but in their conflict with fate. The poem is precisely constructed and demanded a similar precision in the music.

In 1923 Křenek's *Zwingburg* was performed at the Berlin

Opera, and here again the actions of the characters do not provide the main interest, but their opposition to their appointed fate. Křenek entitled the work ' a dramatic cantata,' thus emphasizing his departure both in form and content, from normal opera. The characters have no names. They are called ' The Organ Man,' ' The Man,' ' The Woman,' and ' The Announcer.' It is thus made clear that they are not individuals, as are the heroes of most operas, but types which only stand out for a moment from the surrounding mass. *Zwingburg* (The Castle of Compulsion), is a factory, and the problem is the tyranny of the machine which forces men to keep time to its beat.

As we look back on these works, both libretti and music, we can see how far they reflect all the experiences of the War and the time immediately after it. This was also true of productions of old operas in this period. I remember seeing a performance of *Fidelio* in a town in the Ruhr about this time. The prisoners in the first act were not the usual grey-beards, creeping from their cells with the stock theatrical gestures, but young men with workmen's caps, imprisoned for revolutionary ideas. All the new works of this period had something in common, whether they were concerned, like *Prinzessin Girnara* with a religious problem, or, like *Zwingburg,* with a social one. There was in them all something of the present day, either directly represented or disguised in a historical dress. Or else, in comedy and grotesque, the times were shown in a distorting mirror. It was the old story, discontent with existing theatrical conditions and a desire for a new approach to the public. Only the decisive impulse to the creation of a new style was lacking, until, as I have said, the Handel performances came to fill the gap.

In the first phase of opera the chief characters were represented as figures in a crowd, which, destiny-like, controlled their actions. Now, however, the chief characters were isolated from the crowd, which provided an accompaniment to their actions in a carefully moulded and stylized manner.

It may be that I have a personal reason for considering so

important the effects of the Handel renaissance in creating a
new style of production, quite different from the old. For
these efforts created a perfect setting for the production, in
Mannheim, of my second opera *Alkestis*.

In 1922, when I was adapting Hofmannsthal's *Alkestis* as
a libretto, my aim was to carry on the Viennese tradition from
the last point of contact with ancient mythology, that is to
say from Gluck. It was no mere chance that led me to choose
a mythological subject. In the ancient world I find a quality
of lasting beauty, able to assume a new form in every age. I
had in mind a new synthesis of voices, chorus, ballet and
orchestra, in which the part of the music was to suggest the
fundamental character of a scene, without losing itself in
detail. This could be guarded against by remembering that
the representation in the music of the action on the stage is
always more important than rich orchestral colouring. The
result was a natural musical structure for the whole work,
corresponding to the new style of production in which singers
and chorus aimed at giving every movement a plastic form
which corresponded to the music. The whole stage, from the
protagonists to the last walker-on, was alive, as in a ballet.

Two operas produced in 1925 and 1926, Berg's *Wozzeck*
and Paul Hindemith's *Cardillac* represent another attempt to
restore form in the old sense, to opera. Different as they are in
style and character, they have one thing in common: both
bring to opera forms taken from the symphony and the suite.
The musical material of Hindemith's work is the more accessible, but from the dramatic point of view, he chose the more
difficult task. His music, particularly that of the solo parts,
moves on an entirely different plane from the action. He
accompanies the events on the stage, without ever allowing a
complete union between action and music to take place. Berg
took his forms from absolute music but, as a born dramatist,
he knew how to use them so well that they adapt themselves
perfectly to every movement of the action, and the audience
never realizes that he is using a dance form or a passacaglia,
or writing an act in symphonic form.

Let us now turn to comic opera. Here there are two tendencies. One continues the tradition of the old comic opera, the other uses the representation of modern life on the stage. It is this latter which interests us here.

It was about 1926 that the so-called 'Topical Opera' began to develop in Germany. Like the serious opera it received a considerable stimulus from the renaissance of the stage, from the ballet and from the conversion of the opera singer into an artist capable of controlling his movements as well as his voice. When Tairoff made his tours through Europe we saw to what a pitch of perfection this could be brought by the Russian theatre. Between 1924 and 1930 something similar was to be found in the German theatre.

I have already referred to Rudolf von Laban and his theory of expressive dancing. As teacher, theorist, and organizer he propagated his theories, and founded schools of dancing in many places. The smaller ballets of Stravinsky and Milhaud were performed, and music which seemed suitable for dancing was provided with a choreography. In 1924 Hindemith wrote his ballet, *Der Dämon*, for chamber orchestra, and asked me to revise my *Persisches Ballett* for a small orchestra. Both works were to be given at the Donaueschingen Music Festival.

The appointment, in 1924, of Max Terpis, a pupil of Laban, as maître de ballet at the Berlin State Opera was a great step forward for the new school. Other theatres did not allow themselves to be outdone by the leading opera houses, and the years that followed are marked by an increased interest in ballet. The hitherto conventional ballets of the old operas of the repertory were revised, and in cases where the existing corps de ballet was too small young pupils were brought in from outside to supplement it. They often gave their services for nothing, glad to act as pioneers of the new movement.

These possibilities suggested to me, if I may speak again of my own work, the composition of a work demanding the collaboration of all the elements of the operatic stage. This was my *Opferung des Gefangenen* (Sacrifice of the Prisoner, 1926), after an Aztec ballet-drama dating from the period before the Spanish Conquest. This is, I believe, the most consistent attempt to combine opera and ballet.

The most notable modern satirical opera was *Jonny spielt auf* (Johnny plays the Fiddle) by Ernst Křenek. It was first performed in Leipzig in 1927, and afterwards on other stages. Everywhere, it gave rise to much discussion. In it Křenek made an extensive use of jazz rhythms, not stylized as Stravinsky had done so cleverly in *Ragtime,* nor used as Milhaud had used them in *Saudades de Brasil,* but deliberately and exaggeratedly banal, as in popular dance tunes, and intended as deliberate satire.

An investigation of the reasons for the success of *Jonny* would be an interesting subject for sociological research. Probably no one was more surprised by it than Křenek himself. To write a ' nigger-opera,' as he was everywhere accused of having done, had never occurred to him. He wrote at the climax of the ' prosperity-cry ' period, when material success was enormously overrated, and he managed to express this attitude on the stage in the person of a negro with great success. He seemed, indeed, to share it himself. Then misunderstanding followed on misunderstanding. A negro on the stage was in itself a sensation, just as Monostatos had been in *Magic Flute.* A car on the stage and the railway station scene gave the plain man the thrill of feeling that this was a historic moment in the development of the theatre. The old regime is over, sings the chorus, the new era of success and activity is beginning. Křenek had been considered as an out and out ' modern ' composer, difficult to understand. When therefore, *Jonny* appeared and was intelligible to everyone, people who until then had had no knowledge of modern music, thought that in understanding *Jonny* they showed themselves capable of understanding the whole modern tendency.

To recall them to their senses needed a work which appeared a little later; the *Oedipus Rex* of Stravinsky. Unfortunately he had, on this occasion, oversimplified the problem. Opera-oratorio is no solution. The situation seemed very critical to those concerned with the fate of opera. But at the last moment a rift appeared in the clouds, though in an unexpected quarter. The situation was saved by the *Drei Groschen Oper* (Beggar's Opera) by Brecht and Kurt Weill. This was a topical work with a political tendency. It was not addressed to the opera-going public, but was given night after night in an ordinary theatre by actors who could sing, not by opera-singers. It was no flirtation with opera but a mixture of spoken dialogue and songs of a definitely popular kind.

The *Beggar's Opera* made any continuation in the direction of *Jonny* impossible. It is true that a large number of composers began to concentrate on this type of opera and that many producers tried to introduce the popular revue style of production on the operatic stage. They even applied these principles to old operas, in the hope of giving them a spurious modern character, but the movement came to nothing.

Of far greater artistic importance than these ' Topical Operas ' were the various chamber operas written for the Festivals at Donaueschingen and Baden-Baden. The most charming was Hindemith's little comedy *Hin und zurück*. The scene opens with an uneventful family breakfast. A letter starts the tragedy, and the man shoots himself, thinking his wife has played him false. Then a sage appears and explains that human life need not always develop from birth to death. It can go the other way round for a change. And the whole action and with it the music(in crab fashion) goes back again to the beginning.

In the field of serious opera, on the other hand, a new work of great interest appeared, a work that is, in some passages, almost breath-taking. This was the *Christophe Colombe* of Darius Milhaud, magnificently produced in Berlin in 1930. Dramatically, this work is a cross between *Boris* and *Oedipus Rex*. A narrator connects the individual scenes of the drama by rhythmic speech accompanied by percussion instruments. The action is made even more intelligible to the audience by means of a cinema screen which shows a kind of spiritual landscape, scenes of the past and present which explain the deeper significance of the action on the stage. In this work Claudel created a new form of libretto, and Milhaud faced the problem of opera seriously and gave a masterly answer. The existence of such a work, performed or not, points to the vitality of grand opera, even at the present day.

Now, I should like to try to give some kind of answer to the question which must have occurred to many. Opera has been a living thing in the past and is living to-day, but has it really a future? In spite of the activity of composers and the efforts of theatre managers are we not at the end of a development? If I have been able to express what I wanted to express you will know what I believe. Opera, I think, is not in its nature a narrow and limited field. A glance at its history shows that its whole nature and form is, and always has been, extremely flexible. Whenever in the past external or internal circumstances have brought it to the end of a particular line of development, a path has always been found which has led to a new flowering. Even in its most modern developments the path of opera has branched in several directions, some of which may well prove blind alleys, but one of which may become the high road of the future. Another point which I hope I have made clear is that opera cannot play the rôle of a casual visitor in the life of a nation. Wherever opera has flourished, it has been accepted as an important factor in the nation's spiritual life. Every effort has been made to give it a permanent place among the activities of the human spirit which are the justification of our civilization. Another thing I hope to have made clear is that the action on the stage in an opera must be intelligible to the public, or the music will fail to hold their interest. Opera in England, therefore, must be sung in English. Only then will it be possible for the whole audience to be united in the action, and to experience, as in the theatre, the emotions of the drama. But opera as an institution cannot hope to arouse real interest unless it is concerned with the works of living men. In every place where opera was and is an essential element of the spiritual atmosphere, there is a line of connection between the past and the present. But it is the present which fulfils the promise of the past, and in the works of the present resides the vitality of opera.

VII

The Idea of the Heroic and Opera

I T M A Y B E asked whether there is any justification for once more taking up the question of the heroic in opera, a question which has been discussed again and again ever since there has been such a thing as opera, since it is the heroic that is the basis of every plot in both serious and tragic opera, and it is always heroes who occupy the foreground and for whom the action only serves as a frame.

Indeed, if critical judgement had not gone so far astray in the present day, if the criteria for distinguishing works of art as genuine had not become so uncertain, if unimportant individual experiences were not regarded as manifestations of the workings of fate, and every blind plaything of chance as a tragic hero, such an undertaking would certainly be superfluous.

But the failure of the modern tragic drama is bound up with this fact, that it is only rarely that the power of fate is to be discerned in the events on the stage, instead of blind caprice and arbitrariness, which are presented as though they belonged to the true sphere of art instead of only to its outmost edges.

This perversion of critical judgement can be seen in the choice of what is regarded as essential when a new work is in question. At present criticism almost always exercises itself on irrelevancies, on questions of technique and virtuosity. And with some apparent reason, since most of the works which are put forward as art can only claim distinction through these irrelevancies; by the intensive development of technical devices, but not by the depth of the idea.

A comparison with painting will make this clear. Poussin, speaking of the artist's task, says that in the first place it depends on the choice of a fitting subject, in the second on the composition, in the third on the way in which the material is treated, and last of all on the colours. The same order holds for opera, but it often seems as if composers relied above all on the colours, the scoring, as if they made no fundamental distinction between the treatment of a serious and a comic subject, as if the principles of structure were almost unknown to them, and they were mainly concerned with the choice of the most effective rather than the most suitable subject.

Indeed, in most operas it looks as though the composer had no preconceived plan but, carried away by a detail and abandoning himself to the sound, had set to work without any preparation.

It is in the relationship of poetry and music that the decisive factor for the existence or nonentity of an opera is to be found. It is not the absolute value of the poetry which decides the matter, nor that of the music. Perfection depends on the composer's knowledge of this secret: how to achieve a balance between both elements. But if this is to be reached the working up of a dramatic sketch into a libretto must be as much a creative act as the composition itself.

It seems, therefore, very strange that composers who write their own texts boast of completing them in a few days. But what they call a libretto is generally an incomplete scheme which a poet would have used as a first sketch.

The dramatic idea must first be disposed in such a way as to be capable of supporting a fully worked out action, every detail of which will be intensified by the music.

Rinuccini, Busenello, Zeno, Pariati, Metastasio, Calsabighi, Quinalt, and da Ponte, the great masters of their age, all produced poems which were complete in this sense, and which were sure of a sympathetic reception from the public, so that it depended on the ability of the musician whether the opera was a masterpiece or only a work of talent. A complete failure was practically ruled out, for the composer was so protected by the layout of the poem and by well proved rules and traditions, that the great musician could concentrate on his proper task of giving the piece life and complete realization, while even the merely talented were sure of writing something which would be suitable for the stage.

One thing is apparent in all these poems. The material is raised above every-day life and increased in stature by the omission of detail. But nowadays the artist is so much concerned with the detailed exposition of character, a last remnant of the romantic love of psychologizing, that he has forgotten to think of a higher criterion, the well-balanced relationship of form and content. The sense of form, indeed, is so far lost that it has become an empty vessel in the hands of the untalented. That the work of art can only make its effect as a whole is almost forgotten.

The heroic figure is not dependent on any particular time. He gives expression to ideas which are universal, living forces. Above him is set fate which determines the course of his life. Nothing that touches him can be the mere arbitrary effect of chance.

Raised above the common experience the fulfilment of his destiny becomes a parable, he himself a pattern. The representation of the heroic being on the stage is therefore, if we accept Schiller's view of the value of the theatre as a moral institution from which the spiritual inspiration of a nation flows out as though through subtle veins, the most important function of dramatic art.

There will never be more than a few plots which can support such a representation, but in all ages they are taken up afresh and put on the stage in a new light. The further the poet contrives to depart from any particular time or historical context, the more he will penetrate to the basic forms, to the myths, the clearer his representation will be, and the more suitable for treatment as music drama. It is thus no mere chance but the perceptive power of genius that led Gluck and Wagner in their mature work back to the myth in its oldest and simplest form.

When the poet brings on to the stage the great figures of myth, or of history where the actual happening attains the stature of myth, the air around them is heavy with great events. It is not the fate of the historical individual which moves the spectator. It is the conflict of the hero with the fate that rules him, and that repeats the same patterns through the ages, so that a single form can be glimpsed behind the changing figures; the fundamental form of the myth.

Understood in this way the action cannot be thought of in the modern perverted sense as a mere sequence of incidents, but as the great moment which brings the hero face to face with the fate which is imposed on him. The beginning and end of the drama are equally pre-ordained, as in Calderon's *Great World Theatre,* when the Master dresses the unborn souls as actors, and where it does not matter what rôle they are given to play, but what they make of it. What matters is the attainment by the hero in his struggle with fate of the ripeness which is all; his spiritual growth through this transformation. In opera it falls to the share of the music to give expression to, and to illuminate, this change in the hero.

Thus, to turn to my own operas, the fate of the lovers in *Wunder der Diana* is settled from the beginning. In *Prinzessin Girnara* the action is nearly over when the drama begins, and its course shows the gradual attainment of ripeness by the two main figures—Girnara through the acceptance of her fate, the Prince through the transformation which she has undergone—and both are carried beyond the sphere of common life.

Here it is from the woman that the impulse towards such a transformation goes out, but in *Alkestis* both husband and wife are equally responsible in rising above the all-too-human, and, through a high sacrifice winning the consecration to a higher life. And in *Achill auf Skyros* it is the awakening of the heroic itself which makes of the dreaming, childishly

trifling Achilles, absorbed in a first love, the man who in
the frenzy of the sword dance forsees his fate to the bitter
end and, in full knowledge, accepts it.

Finally, in the *Opferung des Gefangenen* the action is
narrowed down to the moment of crisis. From the beginning
the spectator is fully aware of the fate which will overcome
the hero, but in this great ritual of death the tension arises
from the spectacle of the hero at grips with his fate, when,
in the dances, he undergoes the temptation of life, when all
that makes life worth living is for the last time conjured
up for him and beyond the enchantment remains the cer-
tainty of death from which there is no escape. Through this
he rises to complete self-conquest and becomes one with his
fate.

The representation of the heroic on the stage seems to be
the only means of checking the process of disintegration
which can be seen at work in the last few decades, and of
reawakening the feeling for scale in art. Art has been given
over for too long to the display of the distortions of the
everyday world, the amateurish reproduction of a half-lived
life. Everywhere there has been promise, nowhere fulfilment,
and the measuring rod of positive values has been so far
forgotten that experiment has been preferred to mature work
and the intention of the artist has raised more interest than
his achievement.

But the representation of the heroic rules out the casual
approach, the rhapsodic evasion of essentials, and it demands
the mastery of structure. And the task is most completely
fulfilled when the spectator feels the same sentiment; as the
chorus after the exequies of Mignon says:

' Go, go, back into life. Take with you a holy seriousness;
for seriousness, the holy, alone transforms life to eternity.'

VIII

Alkestis

I CANNOT HELP feeling a certain hesitation in discussing my own work. For words can only too easily cause misunderstanding in the mouth of an artist who speaks of his own work. A work of art is the final formulation of that which its author is compelled to express. Every additional word is, of necessity, imperfect, an irrelevant paraphrase of what has already received its final stamp.

I want, therefore, to talk not so much about my music as about the drama itself, or rather the characters of the drama, about the fate which rules their lives and determines their actions. This approach will give you a more direct insight into the world from which they come, and it will remain for your judgement to decide, when you have seen and heard the drama of Alcestis, how near the composer has come to the realization of his plan.

The myth of Alcestis; of the woman who sacrificed her life to save her husband from his appointed death, has always attracted opera composers. In the last resort there are only a limited number of plots in the whole of dramatic literature, but these are continually rehandled, and the more essential drama is to an age, the nearer to the original myth is the material which the poet takes as the basis for the presentation of the figures which have been transmitted by this material, and their fate.

It will not therefore seem strange that a poet of our own day, Hugo von Hofmannsthal, made a new version of the drama of Alcestis, and that I took up once again this story,

which had received a masterly treatment in the hands of
Gluck more than a hundred and fifty years before.

It is the nature of the stories which the Greek poets have
left to us that many different facets are contained in them,
so that every age can turn to that in which it may see its
own experience as in a mirror. And the characters of these
dramas only take their place among our permanent posses-
sions, only remain alive, because each age has formed them
afresh, and so filled them with its own life.

The *Alkestis* of Hugo von Hofmannsthal is such a re-
creation. The poet called his work a ' Tragedy after Euripides.' If, however, the Greek drama is compared with that
of the modern poet, it is clear that Hofmannsthal handled
the material very freely. With a miraculous instinct the young
poet found the way back to the sources of the drama, to
the stratum of myth from which it grew, and tried to prune
it of later accretions, until it took the form which lies
behind the drama of Euripides.

The nineteen-year-old poet did not fully succeed in carry-
ing out his purpose, and to begin with he only published a
fragment of his version which broke off in the middle of
the play. It was only later, under pressure from his friends,
that he produced the whole drama, in the final part of which
he followed Euripides more closely than in the opening scenes.

I should like to recall to you, in a few words, the content
of the *Alcestis* of Euripides.

It was foretold to Admetus, Prince of Pheres in Thessaly,
that he must die young. But Apollo, who loved him, obtained from the Fates the promise that Admetus should
live long if anyone could be found to die for him. No one
can be found. Then Alcestis, Admetus's young wife,
announces that she is ready to sacrifice herself. The appointed
day comes. Apollo tries in vain to persuade Thanatos to
forgo the sacrifice of Alcestis. Thanatos insists on his right.
An old slave woman appears and tells the chorus how
Alcestis has prepared for death, and taken leave of her
children. Then Alcestis appears, supported by Admetus. She

takes leave of him, of the light, of the earth, of life, and dies.
Admetus commands the whole people to mourn for her, and
the chorus begins the lament for the dead.

Suddenly Heracles stands among the people. He is on his
way to achieve a new adventure. Admetus conceals his
sorrow and receives Heracles in his house. Now the old father
of the Prince appears. Admetus repulses him and reproaches
the old man for not having been willing to sacrifice the few
days of life that remain to him to save Alcestis. The father
accuses his son of having murdered his young wife. Meanwhile the mourning procession assembles, and leaves the
house with the body of Alcestis.

An old servant appears. He is scandalized that Heracles
demands food and drink. Heracles, who has followed him,
asks the reason for his anger. He learns what has happened
in the house of his host. He throws away the garlands which
he had bound round his head and rushes out to make the
descent into Hades, and wrest his prey from Death.

Admetus returns from the tomb, alone to the lonely house.
He laments that he accepted the sacrifice of Alcestis. Then
he sees Heracles return with a veiled woman. Heracles asks
him to keep her in his house until his return from Thrace.
Admetus refuses; his house is dedicated to the memory of
Alcestis alone. Heracles draws back the veil, and Admetus
sees Alcestis standing before him : Heracles has won her
back from Thanatos. But she has not yet recovered the power
of speech. Three days must pass before she will be as she was
before. Admetus receives from Heracles the reward of his
heroic hospitality, and the chorus praise his good fortune.

This treatment of the material by the Greek poet in his
old age could not satisfy the young Hofmannsthal. This is
particularly clear in his handling of Admetus. He is no longer
the Prince of Euripides, who will, in the future, inherit his
father's royal power, but the actual ruler. Behind the drama
of Euripides he saw the older layer, in which Alcestis died
not *for* the beloved husband but *instead of* the King, and

this death is a full death from which there is no return. Such a treatment of the story as a tragedy, however, presupposed the belief of archaic Greece in the appeasement of the Gods by human sacrifice. This solution was already out of keeping with the age of Euripides; it was impossible for a poet of the present day. But the archaic story gave him the key to the problem.

The sacrifice of Alcestis must not be demanded for a human being, even the most dearly beloved, but for the guardian of the people, the chosen of the Gods, of whom it is said in the play that men look up to him and know that:

> If he leads us through fire
> It's well, for he bears helm and shield of the Gods,
> And if he slays, it is as though a lightning flash
> Came indirectly from a God's own hand.

And who can say of himself:

> It is enjoined me
> To be so kinglike that, in this,
> I can forget all my own sorrow.

This is no weakling, desirous of preserving his own life, but one of the race of rulers, on whom kingship is imposed by the Gods. Thus the sacrifice is made for a sacramental power, for something beyond and ruling over humanity, and, in being restored to its original form, the figure of Admetus is raised to a higher level.

No one may accept the sacrifice of another's life; this must then be he whose life is above all other lives, the bearer of royal power which is not his choice, but which the Gods have ordained him to wield.

Alcestis is of equal stature. She is a woman capable of one great act, the sacrifice of her life. Mother and wife, clinging to the beauty of the world, she chooses death so that the King may live. And she prepares for death as for a great ceremony, in which her life is consummated.

In the case of Heracles, as in that of Admetus, Hofmannsthal had to find the way back into archaic Greece. It is the young victorious god Dionysus who passes through the world behind this mask, and before him 'blows a wind of wonders hither.'

He enters the palace and, untroubled, takes food and drink in godlike excess. Excess is characteristic of Heracles; his greed for food and drink, his boisterousness, but also the power to settle everything at one stroke, and to take upon himself the most difficult enterprise, that of wresting the sacrifice from Death. It is the Lord of the dark mysteries himself who speaks to the old slave :

> But if the dead came back,
> They would have eyes still far more full of wonder,
> So full crammed inwardly with wonders
> With limitless desires and with black flames
> Like diamonds which lavishly give back by night
> The light of day they fed on.

In the drama of Euripides the chorus is used as well as the three main characters. Here Hofmannsthal made the most far-reaching structural changes. The strophes of the chorus are to a large extent either replaced by new ones, altered or cut out altogether. The sharp outlines of the separate scenes are softened by connecting passages. For example the entrance of the dying Alcestis is prepared by the chorus as is the approach of Heracles and his return from Hades.

In this way the loose sequence of scenes of the original is welded into a unity and the tension which is felt from the first moment is only resolved at the return of Heracles with the veiled Alcestis.

When I decided to set Hofmannsthal's *Alkestis* to music it was clear to me that the musician must go further on the way pointed out by the poet, and, even more than the poet, must keep the action clear of clogging incident. Thus the dialogue between Apollo and Death which formed the Prologue, and the scene between father and son disappeared. Above all, the scope of monologue and dialogue had to be restricted throughout in order to give the music more space.

Hofmannsthal, occupied with important work, could not himself rewrite the drama, which he had intended for the

ordinary stage, as a libretto. But he sketched out the first
scenes, to show how he considered the revision should be
done, and left me to finish the work.

This stage, the preparation of the libretto, is the most
important and the most fruitful for the opera composer. It is
difficult to describe what goes on in the mind of the composer at this point, for most of it takes place on the threshold
of consciousness. In this preparatory phase the musical atmosphere of the opera is created, though this atmosphere is not
necessarily condensed into music. It is rather that a space
is created between the scenes, between the speeches of the
characters, to be filled at a later stage with music which
elicits the tension between the characters.

The characters of the drama themselves come alive to the
musician, and he lives with them. He sees them, hears them.
They reveal themselves to him and he can follow the course
of their lives. He is concerned in their fate. But more than
this, since he has to direct the course of their lives and actions
through his music, it is clear to him that this music must
be not merely the expression of the immediate speech or
event but must express the given moment as a part of the
whole drama. The greatest economy of means, the suggestion
of what could not be said in words, indications rather than
direct revelation, were essential here.

The greatest problem was set by the treatment of the end,
which Hofmannsthal in his sketch had taken over from Euripides. After the radical changes which Hofmannsthal had
made, the return of Heracles with the motionless Alcestis,
seemed to me to offer no solution from the dramatic point
of view. And Heracles' explanation of the terrible circumstance that only after three days would she regain the power
of speech, did not relieve the situation. We feel that Heracles'
heroic deed, the descent into Hades and the struggle with
Death, is unreal to us if we cannot see and hear the results
of his action. Here the musician must go further than the
poet. There is a solution for him which would be impossible
in spoken drama. I visualized the scene, and then I knew

what was needed. Alcestis stands motionless, like a dead woman. Admetus does not know whether a corpse has been brought back to him or his wife restored. Then the children come through the door of the Palace. They are the bridge to life. The fixed gaze of Alcestis falls on them. A tremor passes through her body. She stretches out her hands to Admetus and a wordless song streams from her lips, growing stronger and stronger. Then it breaks off and softly at first, then more and more strongly, she utters the name ' Admetus,' followed by an exultant outcry, and Admetus joins his voice to hers. But attention must not be concentrated too long on the reunited pair; the saviour must be thought of. Therefore the joy of the chorus finds expression in a paean in praise of Heracles, and a dance like that which his devotees must have performed in honour of Dionysus at the mysteries. And with this the drama ends.

This treatment of the text in long scenes with the omission of all detail determined the general lines of the music. It was necessary to build in large contrasting blocks, and not to lay too much weight on the details of word and phrase. Such music had to be constructed on large lines, full of sustained tension in the opening scenes, lyrical in the scenes between Alcestis and Admetus, light and rapid in the first of Heracles' scenes, but later powerful and tragic, changing finally at the end, with rising intensity, to a hymn of jubilation.

The content gave an opportunity for orchestral interludes with mime and choral singing in the scene of the lying-in-state of Alcestis, and the orgy of Heracles, as well as for a symphonic interlude to bridge over the gap between the departure of Heracles to win Alcestis back from Death and the return of Admetus from the funeral ceremonies.

All this led to the tripartite form in which the opera is cast; first, the Prologue, the death of Alcestis and the lying-in-state; secondly the appearance of Heracles, the drinking scene and the dialogue with the old slave; and lastly, after the interlude, the final part, the mourning scene of Admetus,

the return of Heracles and the re-awakening of Alcestis to
new life, and the final chorus.

I tried to make each scene, as far as possible, a self-contained whole with a characteristic stamp, without, however,
arriving at too artificially isolated, non-dramatic forms, or
at the older forms of opera, which would have been out of
keeping with the serious subject of the drama.

In the opera, as in the play, there are three characters,
Admetus, Alcestis and Heracles, concerned in the action. And
all three attain a higher life as a result of action carried
through by force of will in the teeth of fate : all three undergo
the miracle of transformation.

Fate rules above them, but through the will they are
carried to the act which overcomes fate. Alcestis grows beyond
her ordinary self to the sacrifice of her life. Admetus attains
the most complete spiritual development in his full acceptance
of the kingship divinely imposed on him. Heracles achieves
the most heroic possible deed.

When he brings back the veiled woman to the husband
the terrors of the conflict have made him another man, and
Alcestis, as Heracles had prophesied in his drunkenness, is
not the same, but is one who has seen the world of the dead.

These figures are set in the frame of a solemn ceremonial :
the death, the lying-in-state, the lamentation, the burial. This
gives the composer an opportunity to use mime and choral
dance, so that the orchestra can still speak when the singing
is over. The addition of the final chorus, which, in this position, as in the Greek drama, forms a counterpart to the
mourning chorus, provides the appropriate ending.

In so far as I have succeeded in making clear to you how
the opera took form and shape in my mind, you will understand what I aim at in the performance. It should present a
sharp outline rather than a *clair obscure*, strong contrasts
rather than meticulously worked out detail, and should fix
the emphasis on the stage, not on the orchestra. But at this
point the composer must be silent and leave his work to speak
for itself.

IX

Opferung des Gefangenen

I N T H E *Neuen Deutschen Beiträgen,* Hugo von Hofmannsthal published an old Mexican dance-drama in a translation
by Eduard Stucken. It was chosen for inclusion in this collection not because of the interest of the milieu in which the
action took place, but because of the exceptional quality of
the play, whose poetry stood for something unique and yet
also represented a whole tradition. It was this which immediately attracted me to the drama; and more than this, here
was the possibility of going further on the way already begun
in *Alkestis.*

This will be easily understandable if, as a preface to this
note, I quote the remarks with which Eduard Stucken introduced his translation :

The drama springs up, an opulent blossom, in the age of
Aeschylus, out of the darkness of the past. We know that there
must once have been buds, where blossoms were, but we cannot
see the beginnings of the drama. We cannot see them even in the
India of Kalidasas where architectural style and sculptor's art point
clearly enough to the dissemination of Hellenism. Nor in China,
inundated by the Buddhism of India, nor in its daughter-country
Japan, where old drawings and wood-cuts already bear witness to
a late, sophisticated drama. Nor was the Passion-play of the West
a beginning. The poets of the Miracle plays only spun out the
threads which had never been severed from the time of Seneca
and Plautus. But in the masked dances of the American Indians,
the first steps towards drama can be seen, though the dialogue of
the masks has a liturgical, and not yet a dramatic content. This,
as I see it, is the great value of this strangely beautiful poetry
which I am now laying before a wider audience. It is a beginning,
and it is already drama. More primitive than the first Greek

tragedy it is yet, like it, also an end. For, since it arose, in about the fourteenth or fifteenth century, the Spaniard Alvaredo, the friend of Cortez, passed through Guatemala, hanging and burning. No blade of grass grew again where he had trodden, and what had been in bud never flowered.

We have to thank a strange chance that this Mexican tragedy was preserved for us. A French missionary, the Abbé Brasseur, was sent to the town of Rabinal in Guatemala. Through his skill in medicine he saved the life of an old Indian called Bartolo Ziz. In gratitude the drama, which had not been performed for a generation, was meticulously studied and ceremoniously performed. Brasseur then published the text, with a French translation, as an appendix to his *Grammaire de la langue Quichè, suivie d'un vocabulaire et du drame de Rabinal-Achi*, Paris 1862. Thus this drama—which, certainly, no one would have looked for in a grammar of a Mexican dialect—would have remained in oblivion if Eduard Stucken had not discovered it, in the course of his researches into the speech and culture of Mexico, in a book only accessible to specialists on South America, and, among a multitude of tedious accessories, had not recognized the value of the poetry.

In the original drama the actual dance-play is preceded by a scene in which the hero is taken captive by his enemies on the field of battle. Such a scene might be justified in that heroic age and country where the actor could arouse admiration by the skill with which he handled his weapons, but such naturalistic battle scenes, given at length on the stage, usually mean very little to us to-day. Here especially, however, this scene would have diminished the effect of the stylized war-dance which follows in the main part of the action, where it forms a climax. This first scene, therefore, was, with good reason, omitted in Stucken's version.

In this concentrated form, however, freed from tedious repetitions, the true quality of the poetry reveals itself in all its power. Let us recall the words of Eduard Stucken who, in his prose epic, *Die weissen Götter* (The White Gods) left a moving memorial to the heroic fall of the Mexican race:

*'Die Opferung
des Gefangenen'
Egon Wellesz,
Magdeburg ;
Bühnenbild ;
Aravantinos*

This poem is unique; but that is not the only cause of its magical charm. It is heroic, and it has a bitter scent like the fruit of another planet; a strange sharp fragrance drifts to us from it. The dying hero takes leave of the precious things of the world, of wife, mountains, and valleys. No sentimentality diminishes the heroic mood. Yet a glimmering light of melancholy plays over this drama, as over all old Mexican poems, one of which ends its strophes with the refrain:

' For this abundance of shifting pleasures and splendid joys is like a garland of flowers, which passes from hand to hand and whose beauty vanishes and fades with its life.'

The adaptation of this play for the opera stage meant a further concentration of the dramatic elements, a reduction of all that was episodic and that slowed down the development of the action. Since the five principal dances formed the central part of the drama it followed that the main figure, the captured Prince, could not be a singer, but must be represented by a dancer. For, although some singers are capable of performing rôles involving some dancing, the task which is imposed on the performer here goes far beyond the mere ability to dance alone; the performer must be capable of taking part in the most various combinations and groupings, a capability which cannot be expected of any singer.

I arrived, therefore, at the form used for the *Sacrifice of the Prisoner* by an inevitable necessity, and it was a form in which the essential quality of the poetry seemed to me to be brought into complete harmony with the needs of the opera stage. The speeches and replies of the main characters, the captured Prince and his adversary, the victorious King, are given partly to single figures among their followers, partly to the chorus. This actually has an historical basis. From the Spanish accounts of the Conquest of Mexico and Peru it appears that the Kings considered it beneath their dignity to speak to their enemies and inferiors, but gave their orders by signs. But such historical considerations had nothing to do with the choice of this particular dramatic form; I had no intention of reproducing the Mexican colouring and background. On the contrary it must be emphasized that the original milieu was only retained because the idea of a great and heroic civilization is usually associated with it, so that it can be relied on to lead the imagination of the spectator into certain definite channels. But in so far as the speeches of leaders and chorus are used as they are in tragedy before Aeschylus, the action is raised beyond any single period and given universal application. We are not concerned only with these captives, whose fate is now consummated; with the separation of the speeches from the heroes the action ceases to concern the fate of individuals, and becomes typical. It becomes, too, a ritual, whose separate phases are completed according to sacred usage. Victory and defeat are appointed by fate, and the vanquished must be sacrificed to the gods. It is thus now, and it was always thus. As in the poetry of Pindar the hero stands as the representative of his tribe, his race, and his country. As in the *Epinikia* the deeds of his ancestors are felt behind the deeds of the individual, the *mythos* of his race.

In the face of death the hero reaches his full stature. Still, for the last time, life conjures up all the splendour of the world before his eyes; but he remains unmoved before its enchantment. He knows that his fate can only be consummated in death. Acting from the spontaneous impulse which is the ruling power of his life, he strives, like a natural force, as Hölderlin phrased it, ' Back into the All, the shortest course.' He is one with his fate, which was only hostile to him while he had not grown beyond his separate experience to that which is universal. He is, at the same time, ' Sacrificed and sacrificer, symbol and Idea.' Thus it is tragedy in the Greek sense; the reconciliation of the hero and his fate, as the most complete unification of existence. Beyond all the terror of the events, this theme leads to the resolution of the final song ' Go, O bold one, to your ancestors, the brave warriors; the way is prepared for you.'

The drama must be produced in the light of this basic idea. The performer of the main rôle of the captured Prince must, in gesture and dance, hold fast throughout to the heroic line, unbroken and without sentiment. From him it extends to his warriors and fellow captives. It is through his presence that his enemies first feel the greatness of their victory, so that, when the sacrifice is complete, both groups sink on their knees before the deified hero and praise, in prayer, him who has returned to his ancestors.

The composer who chooses the form of the dance drama must have as clear an idea of the choreography of his work as the composer of an opera must have of the combination of words and music. It is the fault of most music for dance-drama that the musician has not pursued this aim up to the last limit of the achievable. Noverre reported, in his *Lettres sur la dance* that he had first shown Gluck the movements of the Scythian dance in *Iphigénie en Tauride,* the steps, the gestures, bearing, and expression of the separate persons. In accordance with this demonstration the music of this impressive scene took shape in Gluck's mind.

In the same way, before I began to compose, I went through *The Sacrifice of the Prisoner* with the dancer Kurt Jooss, whose great dramatic gifts I had learnt to appreciate in the production of my *Persian Ballet.* He showed me the movements of the dance for each of the situations, so that the right relations between mime and dance could be attained, which, especially for the main figure of the captive Prince, needed the most careful consideration.

This attention to the movement on the stage is, I am aware, an unusual thing for the musician. And it will perhaps seem to be a restriction of the creative imagination, a restraint on the free sway of inspiration. But it must be remembered that, in the case of the stage, the composer has perpetually to see that his ideas are in harmony with the organic development of the drama, and that it is not the unrestricted sway of inspiration which is decisive for the full realization of a work of art, but the innate vitality of the form which the composer, within the limits imposed on him by the material, has to bring out and develop.

The dance itself in *The Sacrifice of the Prisoner* is completely dramatic. It is an integral part of the action, as it was in the great religious festivals of the Greeks. By the integration of the dances in the action the chorus is given a higher function. As in the Greek drama it sometimes takes part in the action, sometimes gives expression to the universal law which is the basis of the drama, but which is implied, rather than stated in the action. This sets the producer the problem of utilizing to the full the medium which the new flowering of the dance has brought to maturity; of filling the stage with intensity and life. Stage settings, costumes, grouping of the chorus and music, demand a unified form which must grow out of the spirit of the drama and the rhythm of the music.

I should like to stress this unity of form as the supreme necessity. It means nothing other than the realization, in a dramatic fulfilment of the action on the stage, of all the forces which are implicit in the music. No one element should predominate over the others; neither the orchestra over the scene, nor the production over the clear outline of the dramatic events, nor the stage settings over the movement of the dance. This unity of form is not easy to achieve in a work like the *Sacrifice of the Prisoner,* which uses the choric dance not as an accessory but as an integral, dramatic part of the whole. It requires, from all who take part, a complete surrender to the rhythm of the drama, an understanding of the structure of the action, and of the interrelation of mime and dance. And yet, in the last resort, it is nothing out of the ordinary that is required, only what every theatre aspires to as the ideal of a perfect performance; and the demand for an unremitting co-operation of all the elements of which the work is composed is that of every age to which the opera, and what it has to offer, are considered essential.

This book is set in 11 point Baskerville, a type designed by the calligrapher and printer to the University of Cambridge, John Baskerville (1706-1775) of Birmingham. Baskerville is a classical type-face described as a letter embodying the most precise geometrical proportions with the greatest elegance. Its sharp precision of outline, best seen on a smooth surface paper under ideal conditions of machining, makes it the forerunner of what is now known as the series of ' moderns.'

The present design is the ' Intertype ' version. This book is printed directly from the slugs cast on the ' Intertype ' machine.